# Counseling
# for
# Anger

RESOURCES FOR
CHRISTIAN COUNSELING

## RESOURCES FOR CHRISTIAN COUNSELING

1. Innovative Approaches to Counseling  *Gary R. Collins*
2. Counseling Christian Workers  *Louis McBurney*
3. Self-Talk, Imagery, and Prayer in Counseling
   *H. Norman Wright*
4. Counseling Those with Eating Disorders  *Raymond E. Vath*
5. Counseling the Depressed  *Archibald D. Hart*
6. Counseling for Family Violence and Abuse  *Grant L. Martin*
7. Counseling in Times of Crisis
   *Judson J. Swihart and Gerald C. Richardson*
8. Counseling and Guilt  *Earl D. Wilson*
9. Counseling and the Search for Meaning  *Paul R. Welter*
10. Counseling for Unplanned Pregnancy and Infertility
    *Everett L. Worthington, Jr.*
11. Counseling for Problems of Self-Control  *Richard P. Walters*
12. Counseling for Substance Abuse and Addiction
    *Stephen Van Cleave, Walter Byrd, Kathy Revell*
13. Counseling and Self-Esteem  *David E. Carlson*
14. Counseling Families  *George A. Rekers*
15. Counseling and Homosexuality  *Earl D. Wilson*
16. Counseling for Anger  *Mark P. Cosgrove*
17. Counseling and the Demonic  *Rodger K. Bufford*
18. Counseling and Divorce  *David A. Thompson*
19. Counseling and Marriage  *DeLoss D. and Ruby M. Friesen*
20. Counseling the Sick and Terminally Ill  *Gregg R. Albers*
21. Counseling Adult Children of Alcoholics  *Sandra D. Wilson*
22. Counseling and Children  *Warren Byrd and Paul Warren*
23. Counseling Before Marriage  *Everett L. Worthington, Jr.*
24. Counseling and AIDS  *Gregg R. Albers*
25. Counseling Families of Children with Disabilities
    *Rosemarie S. Cook*
26. Counseling for Sexual Disorders  *Joyce and Clifford Penner*
27. Counseling for Conflict Resolution  *L. Randolph Lowry and
    Richard B. Meyers*
*(Other volumes forthcoming)*

VOLUME SIXTEEN

# Counseling
# for
# Anger

## MARK P. COSGROVE, Ph.D.

## RESOURCES FOR
## CHRISTIAN COUNSELING

—————————— General Editor ——————————

## Gary R. Collins, Ph.D.

WORD PUBLISHING

Dallas · London · Sydney · Singapore

**Library of Congress Cataloging-in-Publication Data**

Cosgrove, Mark P.
    Counseling for anger / Mark P. Cosgrove.
        p.    cm. — (Resources for Christian counseling : v. 16)
    Bibliography: p.
    Includes index.
    ISBN 0-8499-0598-2
    1. Anger—Religious aspects—Christianity.  2. Pastoral
counseling.  I. Title.  II. Series.
BV4627.A5C67  1988                    88-27799
253.5—dc19                          CIP

*Printed in the United States of America*
   0 1 2 3 9  AGF  9 8 7 6 5 4 3 2

# CONTENTS

Editor's Preface                                        7

Introduction                                            9

  1. The Fires Within                         13

  2. Defining Anger and Hostility             25

  3. The Causes of Anger                      43

  4. How Not to Deal with Anger              62

  5. Slow to Anger: Holding Anger Back        73

  6. Expressing Anger Properly                88

  7. Counseling and Anger in Marriage        105

  8. Counseling and Anger in Children        119

  9. Counseling and Anger at Self            135

 10. Counseling and Anger at God                 148

 11. Preventing Anger                            163

Bibliography                                          177

Notes                                                 179

Index                                                 197

# EDITOR'S PREFACE

Books on counseling often deal with issues that the counselor has never experienced personally. Few of us are alcoholics, anorexic, suicidal, facing terminal illness, perpetually anxious or mate abusers, but we encounter these problems in our counseling and read about them in our therapy books.

Anger, in contrast, is one issue that we all have met first hand. As the author of this book is quick to state, anger is a part of being human. At times we have all lost our tempers, lashed out in frustration or silently boiled in rage. Even when we have learned to control anger, we still get mad at times, often with good reason.

Counselees don't often come to talk specifically about problems with anger. People may seek help with marriage problems, child-rearing difficulties, interpersonal conflicts, depression, grief or the pain of divorce, but while these or other counseling issues are being discussed, anger begins to make its appearance—sooner or later. In overt or subtle forms, therefore, anger tends to be woven into most counseling.

I am grateful that Mark Cosgrove accepted my invitation to write on this important subject. Skilled as a counselor, Dr.

Cosgrove also brings an academician's rigor and a researcher's expertise to the increasingly massive professional literature on anger. But the author has not chosen to produce a weighty, scholarly treatise on his subject. Instead, he has written a practical, informative, and helpful book that draws on the research literature and is illustrated by examples that often come from his own counseling experiences.

This book is part of a series that is intended to be practical and helpful. Written by counseling experts, each of whom has a strong Christian commitment and extensive counseling experience, the volumes are intended to be examples of accurate psychology and careful use of Scripture. Each is intended to have a clear evangelical perspective, careful documentation, strong practical orientation, and freedom from the sweeping statements and undocumented rhetoric that sometimes characterize books in the counseling field. Our goal is to provide books that are clearly written, useful, up-to-date overviews of the issues faced by contemporary Christian counselors. All of the Resources for Christian Counseling books have similar bindings and together they are intended to comprise a helpful encyclopedia of Christian counseling.

Mark Cosgrove, the author of this book, is chairman of the Department of Psychology at Taylor University in Upland, Indiana. Author of several previous books, including *Psychology Gone Awry* and *The Amazing Body Human: God's Design for Personhood,* Dr. Cosgrove received his Ph.D. in psychology from Purdue University.

Sometimes counselors encounter fads and passing issues that come to our attention for a while and then fade away. Anger is not one of these issues. Anger is a part of human nature, present almost from the time of Creation, and likely to appear repeatedly within our counseling sessions and without. Dr. Cosgrove's work can give us a better understanding of this old, complex, and ever-present counseling issue. I hope this book will be helpful as you encounter anger in your counselees, in your home or neighborhood, and in yourself.

*Gary R. Collins, Ph.D.*
*Kildeer, Illinois*

# INTRODUCTION

I had many opportunities to observe people's anger, including my own, as I wrote this book. I remember working in a library on chapter 5, "Slow to Anger: Holding Anger Back," when I took a break to get a candy bar. I placed 45 cents in a machine in the library lobby and a candy bar moved obediently forward. But, it stopped short and teetered on the edge of the drop bin. My mouth watered as I fumbled through my empty pockets for more change.

My first reaction was anger, but I did not want to become an example for chapter 5, so I controlled my disappointment. I tried tapping the side of the machine to get the candy bar to drop. It didn't. I hit harder. Still no luck. By now people were staring at me. I was ready to get into a slugging match with the machine over *my* candy bar when I visualized the newspaper headlines, "Author of *Anger* book arrested for killing candy machine." So, I went hungry and finished chapter 5.

To write this book I interviewed dozens of people—children,

teens, and adults—about their angers. I talked to numerous counselors and pastors about the anger problems in their counseling offices. I also spent many hours in biblical and psychological literature, attempting to understand this very common problem of anger. I hope the results are profitable to the counselor and anyone struggling with anger or bitterness.

The important questions in this book are going to involve what anger is and how it should be counseled. In order to answer these questions and produce practical, sound advice for the counseling of anger, chapters 2 through 6 build a foundation for understanding anger biblically and psychologically. Chapter 2 defines anger, and uncovers its component parts of feelings, thoughts, and behaviors. Anger is both a physiological response and a learned response. Chapter 2 will also address the question, is anger a sin?

Chapter 3 explores the causes of and contributing factors to anger. No counseling theory should be developed until the causes of the problem are well-understood. This chapter will summarize the popular theories of anger as well as the biblical view of the roots of anger. Chapter 4 presents the very common but *wrong* ways to deal with anger. Neither blowing up (ventilation of anger), nor clamming up (suppression of anger), is a helpful method in dealing with anger.

In chapter 5, a basis for counseling anger is begun with the concept of being slow to anger. This biblical concept, which finds much support in psychological literature, means to hold anger back, but not in. Being slow to anger provides the solid foundation for a person to learn how to properly express anger. Chapter 6 explains another part of the biblical approach to anger, which also has a wealth of psychological support. Our counselees must learn how to express anger constructively and without sin. The proper expression of anger is essential in mature, loving relationships.

Chapters 7 through 11 put into practical language the counseling of a variety of anger situations from the foundation of being slow to anger and expressing anger properly. Chapter 7 deals specifically with anger in marriage, while chapter 8 addresses anger in children. Chapter 9 offers advice for anger directed against oneself, and chapter 10 concerns anger at God.

All of these types of anger are related and share some of the same counseling principles, but each is also unique and demands some more specific, practical steps for its resolution.

Learning how to express anger once it arises is not the only goal of the counseling of anger. Learning how to prevent anger is a needed step toward developing Christian peace. Chapter 11 suggests many practical ways of anger prevention, including using people in the local church body to counsel and confront. Since anger touches many other problems, counselors need to be well-read in a variety of counseling areas.[1] In addition, counselors should become familiar with more specific topics related to anger such as the ethical and legal aspects of violence.[2]

Reading this book or any book on anger, no matter how well-written, will not change people's angry natures. No sermon, audiotape, or good example to model will change people. One goes from being an angry person to a peaceful person through the deliberate steps of the Christian walk toward maturity in Christ accompanied at times by the practical help and advice from a Christian counselor. The fact that there is no quick fix for anger is not a cause for alarm. Counselors need to be confident that they can help counselees develop healthy responses to anger. Changing from angry people to people of peace takes time and hard work and God's grace. Be skeptical of any quick fix. A sound biblical and psychological approach to anger should give people a sense of hope that they can change, that they can heal their relationships, and that they can begin to enjoy life again.

I am thankful for the excellent guidance and support I have received from Dr. Gary Collins, editor of this series. I refused the temptation to get angry at him for his editorial suggestions. For his part, Gary proved to be mild-mannered and peaceful as he coaxed the best I could do out of me.

My thanks also go to Nancy Gore, who typed the manuscript, and Carey Moore of Word, who edited the book and prepared it for publication. If these people had not been so peaceful and calm under the stress of a deadline, they would surely have become anger examples in the book.

# Counseling
# for
# Anger

RESOURCES FOR
CHRISTIAN COUNSELING

# CHAPTER ONE

---

# THE FIRES WITHIN

Anger may be the most common emotional experience that human beings share. In any one week, not all people feel romantic thrills, or Olympic urges to jog. Not everyone has felt the impulse to rob a bank, or has spent time lusting after a neighbor's property or spouse. Jealousy is rare; fears are a bit more common; laughter is heard only in the good times. The feelings of stress and anxiety depend upon work situations, the traffic, and the number of children in the house. Depression varies with a person's psycho-past and bio-present. But, most people, if they are honest, have had recent feelings of anger. They have shared legions of little irritations, which attacked their joy. For some, anger flashed hot when the Coke machine held them up for loose change. For others, there was an almost unconscious boil at news of the rising price of gasoline. For still others, major arguments with spouse and children have taken place in the home.

Many of the people that a counselor will see are angry people. Their anger this week may reflect the solid mountain of resentment built up over the years concerning their parents, or their appearance, or their bad lot in life. Such resentment may be unconscious, but it is ever-present in their tone of voice, their attitude to others, or their low self-esteem. Their anger this week may have been a specific hatred toward a persecutor at work, or a general racial prejudice invisible to them, but not to others; or verbal disgust over the weather may have been the occasion of their angry outburst. For overworked moms there is no counting the number and types of furies. To be human and doing anything is to be exposed to anger. Even counselors get angry at their clients.[1]

Anger and aggression are more characteristic of humans than animals. Rather than think of the animal world as "red in tooth and claw," it is enlightening to see how animals have many biological and ethological restraints on aggression, whereas humans seem to have none.[2] The biblical warnings against anger seem very appropriate.

I was tempted to fill this book with the typical extreme examples of anger. You have seen the ones I mean in the newspaper: Angry man shoots five bullets into cigarette machine; NBA assesses $15,000 in fines for fights during the basketball playoffs; a man strangles his wife because she put mustard on the wrong piece of bread in his sandwich. In the daily police records of a large city the following "anger" crimes were recorded.[3]

| | |
|---|---|
| noon | A 37-year-old woman and a 62-year-old woman are arguing when the older woman pulls a knife and cuts the younger one. |
| 2:50 P.M. | A 32-year-old man pulls a .22 caliber revolver on his 24-year-old wife as they argue over a pair of socks. |

| 3:15 P.M. | In a nursing home, a 60-year-old mother is confronted by her 27-year-old daughter with a .22 caliber rifle. |
| 4:15 P.M. | A 44-year-old man cuts a 51-year-old man on the ear with a butcher knife at a gas station during an argument. |
| 6:15 P.M. | A 39-year-old woman and a 16-year-old boy argue about whether he can buy groceries on credit. He starts to throw a jar of pickles at her, but she stabs him in his side. |
| 11:00 P.M. | Two men, angry over how a 42-year-old man is treating their mother, drag him out of a bar and pistol whip him. |

Newspapers and psychological literature contain numerous examples of child, spouse, and elderly abuse.[4] Most sources agree that violence in the family is on the rise because family stress is increasing in our society.[5]

A typical historical example of extreme anger was Adolf Hitler. He was said to . . . "lose all control of himself. His face became mottled and swollen with fury, he screamed at the top of his voice, spitting out a stream of abuse, waving his arms wildly and drumming on the table or the wall with his fists."[6] Not long ago, extreme rage was the subject in a piece of popular fiction in which a man, who suffers from psychomotor epilepsy, goes on a killing spree every time he has a seizure.[7]

But we do not need any more of these examples. They may get attention, but they might also distract us from the fact that anger is a problem common to everyone. More than any other element of people's lives, anger affects relationships and happiness. The mass murderer may represent the top of the volcano, but all need to talk about the fires within.

I see anger in many counseling situations. I see it in a man's reaction to his car that regularly needs repair, or in a neighbor's reaction to baseballs landing in her garden. Every day I see two men, who work together, but who have not been civil to each other for years. I know a husband and wife who hide twenty-five years of resentment and indifference behind a polite exterior. I have seen angry neighbors literally and figuratively erect fences that testify to a division as wide as that between the two Berlins. Every counselor has seen the same, and more, angers.

Last week I watched one of my sons' Little League baseball games and saw anger as the ever-present spectator, both in the stands and on the field. The smallest players, in order to play their best, needed the charge of energy that competition and its mock hostility can give. The players were not angry, but they were "enemies." The game was tied and everyone's emotions were high. When the home-plate umpire, who was a high-school student, called a player out, one of the coaches became incensed. This coach, who was physically larger and many years senior to the umpire, stormed over to the umpire, yelling and waving his arms. He loudly reversed the call of the umpire and told the player to get back on base. In Little League there are no professional umpires. The umpires are fifteen-year-olds making ten dollars a game, and they have no provisions for throwing a coach out of a game. The kid-umpire swallowed the abuse and the game started up again. But, the umpire's anger was not gone simply because it was not expressed. I suspect that the umpire felt a secret joy later in the game when he called two close outs at the plate against the angry coach's team. Umpires resist "getting even" I am sure, but we can all empathize with the desire.

The crowd was not nearly as tame as the persecuted umpire. Many parents shouted, "Let the umpire call the plays!" Other parents said that the kid-umpire had made a bad call and should learn more about baseball. Of course, the crowd's reaction depended on whether people saw the call in their team's favor or not. One parent shouted and made an angry gesture at the offending coach. The coach returned the gesture as if to say, "I'll meet you after the game!" I felt my own anger at the abusive coach, who seemed out of control and very rude to a fellow human being. But, I controlled my champion-of-the-downtrodden anger, knowing I had to write a book on the subject and did not want to be one of my own examples. I have to admit that the umpire's call was in favor of my son's team. I wonder how I would have felt if my son had been on the angry coach's team. Amazingly, the opposing coach, who had the most at stake, and perhaps more permission to vent his disapproval, was calm throughout the shouting. Maybe he knew the umpire had made a mistake. Or, perhaps, he had some secret for restraining his anger.

These examples of anger do not suggest that anger is merely an explosive, biological response to the proper stimulus. The anger process may occur rapidly, but, it is not a simple stimulus-response event. People at the baseball game experienced the automatic reactions of rising pulse and rapid breathing, but those reactions depended on who they were and what their thoughts were, and if they felt the need to control themselves because of moral or social dictates. To solve the problem of anger, counselors need to know more about it and why it has such a powerful presence in people's lives.

The clichés we use about anger reveal some information about its nature. Individuals get "hot under the collar" or "do a slow burn" in testimony to the biological reaction they can feel. They are "boiling mad," feel like "exploding," or "swallow" their anger, when they are holding their tempers in for whatever reason. Metaphorical therapies include "counting to ten," "simmering down," or "defusing the bomb" as thoughts become a part of the anger process. Anger has been linguistically called a "storm" and a "high-spirited horse." These metaphors describe what everyone has felt, that anger is a complicated human response. As all of our emotions, anger is composed of biological reactions, thoughts, interpreted feelings, decisions, habits, overt behaviors, and sometimes even subconscious motives.

## MR. SPOCK OR THE INCREDIBLE HULK?

In trying to understand anger the counselor does not need to spend much time looking at myths of anger, such as Mr. Spock, the emotionless Vulcan of the "Star Trek" series, or television's "The Incredible Hulk," representing an uncontrollable force within people. These examples of emotion exist nowhere but in imaginations. Unlike Mr. Spock and full-blooded Vulcans in "Star Trek," emotions, including anger, are an essential part of what it is to be a human being. It is neither desirable nor possible to purge oneself of emotions.

Emotions, including anger feelings, are important to human beings.[8] Without emotions your counselees would experience no joys in life. In addition, thoughts, motivations, and knowledge itself cannot be considered just rational entities, but are highly dependent upon emotional feeling. One can learn as much about the problem of suffering from reading the emotional journal of C. S. Lewis after the death of his wife, as from his rational discourse on the subject.[9] Dieting, jogging, doing homework, confronting injustice, or working eight hours a day all require the motivational charge of feelings such as dedication, love, self-worth, shame, anger, fear, and pride. Rational thought alone will not satisfactorily carry out the garbage, make love or discover a cure for cancer. If humans want to exist on a rational plane, alone, they will accomplish nothing but a depersonalized existence. But, with emotions, including anger, life becomes human.

It is equally misleading, though, to see anger or any emotion as The Incredible Hulk's disease. This view sees a negative emotion like anger as an uncontrollable animal rage that is part of human evolutionary baggage. Biological arousal is a part of anger, but the animal-rage notions serve only to perpetuate the myth that anger cannot be tamed and consequently no one is responsible for it. If anger is merely a biological reaction, people can with impunity retreat into their "hot-blooded" nature or their "Irish tempers" and ruin life for themselves and everyone around them.

## ANGER IN THE COUNSELOR'S OFFICE

Unfortunately, much of the anger counselors encounter is out of control. It is anger that is not thought about, and which does not accomplish most of the goals people might set before themselves. The anger within ourselves or others can vary from irritation and brief displays of temper, to violent rages. The most familiar expressions of anger include the loss of temper, shouting, fighting, hostility, and even physical abuse. There are also hidden angers, which nevertheless manifest themselves in a disagreeable attitude, negativity, cynicism, sarcasm, hostile humor, school-age nicknames, pouting, resentment, and a sullen attitude. Even if these are not the counselees' problems, they are the problems of the people they live and work with. Therefore, they experience anger problems no matter what side of anger they are on.

Angers are complicated in other ways. They relate to who our counselees are as people, their previous experiences, their self-images, expectations, and even their biochemistries.

A father who becomes angry when his wife praises their son is not expressing a simple biological or psychological response. His feelings relate to his own sense of worth, his expectations of his wife, and his current relationship to his wife and son.

A child's anger also differs from an adult's anger. Children move easily in and out of extremes of emotions, crying bitterly one moment, happily playing the next. Part of this relates to children's limited social and personal awareness and their lack of learning patterns to guide their emotions. Counseling problems with anger in children are increasing because of increases in divorce, adoption, and other family-changing circumstances that affect a child's sense of stability in the home.[10] More anger problems also occur in young people's lives as they mature, because their stressors increase with age.[11] Anger problems increase along with the pressures of school, with females and graduate students showing some of the highest indications of anger.[12]

But children soon become mothers and fathers. How does one best characterize a family's anger, which is so constant, so harmful, so guilt-provoking, and yet so understandable and even necessary at times? Counselors will see many women dealing with anger. A mother's anger is not simple, since it is related to her training to stifle her unladylike feelings for fear of alienating others. Many mothers are locked up in their homes, underpaid and underpraised, for sixteen-hour days of manual labor with the constant demands of young children. A mother is prone to anger's dark side, and yet may lack the vehicles for expressing her anger. She feels guilty if she becomes angry on her own behalf, and, therefore, she may express anger about things around her, from leaky faucets to social injustice.

19

Who cannot sympathize with the pastor's anger? The typical pastor has many reasons to feel anger, and yet, because of expectations about pastoral virtue, he (or she) has little freedom to express it. The pastor may be underpaid, work longer hours than most people, accept endless complaints, and also feel the need to conform to every congregational demand.

Counselors will discover that anger is not an isolated personal problem, but it exists as a web among all interpersonal relationships and as a partner in most personal problems. They can help many types of counseling problems by being attentive to the counselees' angers that accompany these problems. Whenever people have interpersonal contacts, anger is a possibility. Anger feelings naturally thread their way in and out of all the family interactions. I say "naturally" because families are groups of separate individuals, with different needs, goals, aspirations, and levels of maturity. Whenever any degree of commitment and interaction in the family is involved, anger-producing situations are inevitable. Thus, many counseling sessions involve anger problems. Even anger directed at the counselor can be a hint of problems that exist beyond the counselee's complaint.[13]

## ANGER AT SELF AND GOD

Feelings of anger are involved in many of the situations that relate to counselees' feelings toward themselves and toward God. A low self-concept is often directly involved with anger at oneself for not measuring up, or for failing or sinning in some way. We often have higher expectations of ourselves than of those around us, because we are continually striving to make up for our perceived lack of self-worth. The increased anger demands we place on ourselves result in more failures and shattered expectations, and more anger at self. This anger becomes a vicious cycle of anger at self, raised expectations, failure, and then more anger at self. Anger at self may be self-defeating, but it is a constant companion to many people with problems of self-esteem.

As with anger at self, people's anger at life or God can leave them feeling dead inside. This anger reacts against the hurts people have received at the hands of fate or God. It is the feeling of being helpless, of having no future, of being locked in; it is an "I don't deserve this" mentality. In its mild form, anger at life or God can lead to self-pity and lethargy. In extreme forms, severe emotional disturbances lead to retreats from life—and suicide becomes the ultimate retreat. Anger at life may be related to midlife crises, singleness, or grief over the death of a loved one. Expressed properly to God, anger is not a problem, as the book of Job illustrates; but anger at life or God that is sad, helpless, and self-pitying can have disastrous effects on human life.

Other common angers that are present in the counselor's office are bitterness, hostility, and resentment. These angers represent an accumulated storehouse of anger, often from childhood, that a counselee lives with. These angers are common even among "good" Christians because Christians have often been taught that anger is a sin and, therefore, should not be felt or expressed. Angry people, therefore, learn to stifle their angers, and do not learn the proper ways for dealing with anger feelings. Year after year such angers at people and life build up and make their explosive appearance later. The task of the counselor is to teach such individuals to recognize their angers and learn to handle them effectively.

## NEGATIVE RESULTS

Anger has the potential to rob people of life's joys because it reaches into every area of their personal and relational lives. Relationships and careers are exciting. Holidays and hobbies are fun. But, when anger is present, these joys are lost. How many Christmas mornings, wedding receptions, and family picnics have been lost to an angry moment? How many of the joys of family and friends do people not experience, because they are irritated, inconvenienced, offended, or otherwise bothered? How many total years of a marriage are lost to shouting, sulking, or embittered silence? How many beautiful days, healthy bodies, or wonderful educational experiences go unappreciated because of unbridled pessimism or bitterness?

People usually seek counseling help for anger not because they recognize their anger problems, but because it is interfering with some aspect of their lives. Some individuals actually like being angry and use it to power their ways over others, or to sulk and punish those who have offended them. Sooner or later, though, joy is bled out of angry people's lives because anger interferes with their needs for affirmation and acceptance. Angry people invite anger and power plays in return. They have developed strained relations with loved ones, and contacts with others are superficial.

John, a college teacher, was hostile and opinionated, quick to blame and criticize his students. He justified his hostility by believing that all students are lazy. Eventually he sought counseling, because his department did not recommend him for tenure. He had apparently offended too many people. Counseling helped John discover that he did not have one satisfactory relationship in his life. The only pleasure he seemed to have was in "lording" it over others, and even that was proving costly. Anger is not free. It was costing John his job and his happiness. But, with counseling help, John learned how to deal with his anger and how to express his feelings. He quickly began to discover a new joy in his relationships at work and at home.

Unresolved anger may be an underlying cause of many physical and emotional problems. People who use anger as a weapon to get their ways and force others to yield are affecting their own lives in many harmful ways. They soon find out that unrestrained hostility can be a costly, life-destroying habit. When angry people clear up the resentments and bitterness in their lives, they resolve many of the other problems they are experiencing, particularly in their relationships. It is not difficult to imagine that marriage problems involve anger, and that resolving the angry communication patterns will aid the struggling marriage. James 3:14 warns against bitterness and selfishness, because they lead to disordered and evil lives. On the positive side, James 3:17, 18 promises that peacemakers will reap a bountiful harvest in their lives.

## Anger and Emotional Health

Uncontrolled and poorly expressed anger wreaks havoc with people's emotional lives. Family life and other close relationships provide occasions when irritations and stresses naturally arise; individual interests, differences, and dissimilar goals come into frequent conflict. If people let anger reign uncontrolled in their relationships they will lose those relationships that are so important to their fulfillment as persons. Unchecked anger between loved ones can grow into bitterness and hostility, and it can eventually lead to physical abuse. Hebrews 12:15 states that bitterness toward others is a root that can "cause trouble and defile many."

### Anger and Personal Peace

The shattering effects of anger on relationships quickly undermine personal peace and well-being. Contentment, joy, and happiness are replaced by hatred and discontent. Rational, ordered thinking can be replaced by self-centered, vindictive thinking. Hot rage leads to the reduction of one's cognitive capacity, ordinary judgment, and the ability to appreciate the complexity of situations.[14] People who are characterized as angry react more often and more intensely to aversive events than do people who don't normally react in anger to life's disappointments.[15] People may walk away from an angry encounter or a humiliating experience, but rehearse the situation over and over again in their minds.

In their mental dialogue they tell off the offending party, or defend their case before unseen jurors. At dinner time, they tell about the day's angry episode and fail to taste the quality of the meal or appreciate the joys of family life. Solomon's wisdom rings a true warning: "Better a meal of vegetables where there is love than a fattened calf with hatred" (Prov. 15:17). Even sleep can no longer be enjoyed. The turmoil of the mind during the day does not leave them when they wish to sleep.

> The man I hate may be many miles from my bedroom; but more cruel than any slave driver, he whips my thoughts into such a frenzy that my innerspring mattress becomes a rack of torture. The lowliest of serfs can sleep, but not I. I really must acknowledge the fact that I am a slave to every man on whom I pour the vials of my wrath.[16]

Having good emotional health is difficult even in the best of circumstances. But in an environment of bitterness, hatred,

23

personal tension, and strained relationships, our emotional health becomes vulnerable to a variety of disturbances. Habitual hostility and the pride involved in anger that "lords" it over others is the opposite of the humble attitude required for spiritual growth. Such hostility clouds people's thinking and leaves them open to Satan's manipulation and lies. Paul warns Christians to resolve their anger conflicts quickly, lest they "give the devil a foothold" on their personalities (Eph. 4:27). The habitually angry person becomes more vulnerable to Satan's temptations, and, therefore, becomes difficult to teach, or to work or live with. Anger interferes with personal growth—particularly any critical feedback that is needed for spiritual growth.

# CHAPTER TWO

# DEFINING ANGER AND HOSTILITY

Anger is an intense emotional reaction all people have felt in response to a variety of situations. Sometimes counselees express this emotion in overt, hostile behaviors. At other times they hold it in. In either case, anger is usually an unpleasant, emotional feeling that is hard to control. This chapter will dissect the emotional reaction we call anger to explore its component parts, so we can better understand its cause and cure. Anger is not a disease, but a problem in living that is neither simple nor easy to change.

## Mom Gets Mad

Most of us can remember our parents getting angry with us, and now, as parents, we can identify with the everyday angers in raising children. Kids seem to know by instinct what to do to make parents, especially moms, angry. My three young sons are model examples of what children are like in this regard, so much so that when my wife and I stop to consider the things that make us angry, we believe our children's behaviors would make good material for a Bill Cosby comedy routine. There are the endless squabbles: "He's touching me!" "I sat here first!" "Mom, he's looking at me!" There is the passing of gas in the bathtub and burping in sequence during meals. There is the constant, "I dunno. I didn't do it. He did it first." There are smelly, dirty socks under one kid's bed, or the time the youngest was tricked into sitting on a whoopie cushion, and now he is hitting his brothers. There's the time when the hamster got loose, or when someone, or everyone, has missed the toilet again. But we suppose these happen in everyone's home.

To no one's great surprise mom "blows her top." But what is a mother to do? She collects herself before I return home from work and tries to do better. She sets a delicious meal on the table, and then I mention that I do not have any ice in my water. Suddenly, I see the three boys snickering. They are laughing about who got the most green peas and a solitary green pea is being passed back and forth under the table. I retreat into my major responsibilities of worrying about family finances and the current world situation. The kids have ignored their mother all day. Her husband does not help with this or appreciate what she has been through. The kids never like the vegetables she serves. Finally, when the AWOL pea gets tossed across the table and hits mom in the head, the sword of Damocles is dropped.

Mom gets angry, of course, but, she has been angry in a variety of ways all day. She held her anger in and stewed in her mind. She was irritated. She was enraged. She was cool to her husband. She exploded once or twice. She cried. She felt guilty and like a failure as a mother. Like thousands of other mothers, she felt powerless to change.

## THE IMPORTANCE OF DEFINING ANGER

People who are experiencing the uncomfortable effects of anger need to have the answers to two questions before they solve their anger problems. One first needs to answer the morality question. *Is this anger wrong?* Is it a sin? The second question relates to the first. *Is it possible to control anger?* Or is anger an instinctive, biological reaction that rises up and lashes out the moment the anger-producing situation occurs?

Anger certainly feels like a reflexive, irrational response to a threat. Psychoanalytic theories describe anger as a primitive personality state or an irrational response to threat.[1] Bad tempers seem to be out of control, at least at times. How much we can hold those we counsel responsible for their angry outbursts depends upon the answer to our second question: Are people able to control their angers? It is a question of hope, the hope of change. If anger cannot be altered significantly by our counselees' efforts, then they are without hope of eliminating the angry tensions and behaviors that fill their days and plague their relationships. If this is the case, then every mother of young children is doomed to repeat her cycle of anger and guilt feelings. Let us examine and define anger very carefully with the goal of answering the above two questions.

## THE COMPONENTS OF ANGER

A close inspection of anger reveals that it involves both an inner emotional response and an outer behavioral response. Before, during, and after the emotional response, thoughts are occurring which can affect both the inner emotion and the outer behavior. These three components of anger—emotional, cognitive, and behavioral responses—are so intertwined with each other, that people experience the emotion of anger as one continuous surge.[2] This holistic experience of the separate components of anger is the reason that people tend to think of their anger feelings as sin, because they are frequently attached to explosive, hostile thoughts and behaviors. Counselees also tend to lose hope for change, because they lose sight of the thinking and behaving components of anger and focus on the physiological surge of emotional arousal.

When we look at anger as these three component parts blended into one, it is possible to consider that the angry expressions in thought or act may be sinful, but that the anger feelings themselves may not be. It is also reasonable to assume that while the physiological surges that contribute to anger feelings may not be controlled directly by people, the thoughts and behaviors with which they interpret and express their feelings are under control. The harried mother should not feel ashamed about her natural reactions to stress, and she needs to feel confident that she can exercise control over her behaviors in response to anger feelings.

We can easily see the biological component of anger when we look at an infant, for when babies do not get their own ways they become very angry. All babies do. Infants do not have to learn how to get angry, because anger is a natural response to stress and frustration.[3] The feelings of anger are part of a God-designed, internal system to help give people the energy and motivation to accomplish difficult or threatening tasks. Everyone, from infancy on, experiences these general anger feelings without which people would be defenseless in the face of innumerable difficulties in life.[4]

Anger is also a learned response. It may not only be the expression of a feeling but also a learned defense against painful feelings.[5] How people react during periods of emotional arousal depends upon several factors, from how their parents handled their anger to how they interpret the current situations that are provoking them. Considering the negative effects of learning from someone else's anger, Scripture warns us, "Do not make friends with a hot-tempered man, do not associate with one easily angered, or you may learn his ways and get yourself ensnared" (Prov. 22:24–25). Even though anger expression is learned and, therefore, initially under control, this does not mean that people know how to handle their angers. This lack of knowledgeable control in handling expressions of anger leads to the many different expressions of anger that people can show. The anger emotion is a biological state of readiness and tenseness. But, the expression of anger can include feelings of irritation, hatred, self-pity, temper outbursts, thoughts of frustration, low self-esteem, pessimism, or verbal and physical aggression. Anger can be a short temper or a general attitude of hostility to everyone and everything.[6] Anger can be violence.[7] Anger can be competitive arousal. All of these expressions of anger can share the same physiological arousal state, but be a part of a separate learned response.

Learned anger expression is capable of being good or bad. Anger expression can be controlled or changed according to the environment in which people find themselves. Albert Ellis has been successful in promoting the idea that anger can be controlled by its cognitive or thinking component.[8] His ABC's of anger illustrate the components of anger as A, the activating experience; B, the belief system; and C, the consequence or emotional response. According to Ellis, one's belief system (B) determines whether an activating experience (A) will cause an emotional response (C).

Psychologist Richard Walters divides anger into three types based upon differences in cognitive or behavioral components.[9] Rage and resentment are destructive expressions of anger, while indignation is a constructive, loving expression. Each of these three combines physical arousal with different cognitions and behaviors. Rage is violent, uncontrolled anger, whereas resentment is the suppressed feeling of anger that seeks revenge. For Christians who see rage as a sin, resentment becomes a common expression of anger. Both rage and resentment seek to destroy people and are guided by selfishness. Indignation, on the other hand, seeks justice and usually defends some other person. Walters feels that among Christians there is a fear of rage, a surplus of resentment, and a shortage of indignation.[10] Christian maturity in the area of anger involves recognizing and eliminating rage and resentment from one's life and becoming courageous enough to be righteously indignant when the occasion demands.

The Bible uses different words for anger to describe rage, resentment, and indignation. The two most frequently used New Testament words for anger are *thumos* and *orgē*. *Thumos* means a turbulent commotion, an explosion of temper, or rage. It is used approximately twenty times in the New Testament. *Orgē* is a long-lasting attitude that continues to seek revenge. It occurs forty-five times in the New Testament, and may be translated as resentment. A third word, used five times in the New Testament, is *aganaktēsis*. It is translated as indignation and means anger without inappropriate behavior. Whatever its

29

expression, anger is always a powerful emotion. The Old Testament captures this idea by using the word *aph* for both the anger of God and man. *Aph* translated literally means "nostril." This anger word gives us a picture of nostrils flared or snorting during anger.

## A Physiological Response

The feelings people get when they are angry are in part the result of their bodies' physiological arousal to a changing environment. The human chemistry of adrenaline and to some extent noradrenaline are the fuels of anger and many other emotions as well.[11] The body's autonomic nervous system serves during times of stress to "get the adrenaline flowing" by stimulating the adrenal glands to release two hormones, epinephrine (adrenaline) and norepinephrine (noradrenaline), which, in turn, signal a number of other organs to perform their specialized functions. The spleen releases more red blood cells to aid in clotting in case of injury. Bone marrow is stimulated to make more white blood cells to counteract infection. The liver produces more sugar to build up the body's energy. The pituitary gland also secretes two hormones, the thyrotropic hormone (TTH) which stimulates the thyroid gland to make more energy available to the body, and the adrenocorticotrophic hormone (ACTH) which stimulates the release of thirty hormones including the steroids, which are important in many metabolic processes.[12]

Any unfamiliar or stressful event that potentially affects people stimulates the production of adrenaline and noradrenaline. These two chemicals seem to give people the feeling of anger, the arousal, the tenseness, the excitement, the heat. These hormones stimulate changes in heart rate, blood pressure, lung function, and digestive tract activity, which further add to the general arousal feelings people have when they are angry. This strong physiological component of the anger response explains the link between anger and hypertension.[13] The upward surge of these hormones during a stressful or threatening situation does give people the impression, though, of being overwhelmed by anger and without power to control it. It is interesting that even the pitch of a person's voice changes in intense anger depending upon whether one is angry in response to frustration or to threat. The more the frustration the higher the voice pitch.[14]

The physical arousal produced by adrenaline and noradrenaline is not enough to "cause" the emotion of anger. These arousal feelings produced by the autonomic nervous system's response to a threat are vague and difficult to describe. Direct brain stimulation produces similar vague emotional arousal. Patients report feeling "a premonition of imminent disaster of unknown cause" or "a constriction of warmth in the chest."[15]

This general physiological arousal needs a psychological or cognitive component before the person begins to experience the fullness of what we call anger or rage.[16] Some mental interpretation of stressful events is needed before blood pressure or heart rate can be transformed into hostility or resentment. A nurse who is taking care of a patient dying of cancer deals with the rudeness of the patient much better than she handles the rudeness of her husband later that day. Her anger at her husband is a function of her arousal feelings and her cognitive expectations of a husband as opposed to a dying cancer patient.

## A Cognitive Response

When people emphasize their physical arousal feelings during anger, they make statements such as, "I was so mad I couldn't see straight," or "I just got carried away," or "that kid makes me so mad!" These responses hide the fact that there are thoughts occurring prior to and during angry feelings, which thoughts affect anger expression. The body's arousal system may respond to anger-producing situations suddenly and powerfully, but whether people act out their urges or not depends upon their mental interpretation of the events and the appropriateness of certain anger expressions. The total anger response is not a knee-jerk reflex to some environmental stimulus, but a response that is structured by our counselees' concrete ways of thinking about themselves and the people making them angry. Other beliefs that shape anger expressions are the meanings of the situations people find themselves in, their interpretations of other peoples' motives, and their philosophical beliefs about the purposes that pain and suffering may serve.

Acknowledging the cognitive component in the anger response may give rise to guilt feelings, because thinking implies control over anger. Depression often correlates with anger feelings because of underlying guilt feelings.[17] But, if the mind is a major component of the anger response, then there is hope that hostility, temper, bitterness, and irritability can be changed.

At the physiological level all emotions are very similar. While there are some minor physiological differences between anger, fear, joy, or romantic passion, it is the cognitive component of an emotion that determines what the experience will be. Many experiments have been able to demonstrate that a generalized arousal biology can result in a variety of emotional states depending on the person's cognitive interpretation of the situation.[18] The mind interprets signs of physiological arousal and feelings of anger are the result. If for any reason people's mental perceptions of the situations change, they are vulnerable to a rapid shift in emotions, because their physical arousal is already high. An angry wife is about to throw an expensive vase at her husband, but, remembering its value, she rolls it on the floor at him instead. They both explode in laughter. The biological arousal remained the same, but the cognitive appraisal of the situation changed and a new emotion was powerfully experienced. In other words, the body's arousal combines with a specific mind-set, which together give rise to a chosen, behavioral expression of what people think they are feeling.

## A Behavioral Response

The behavioral response in anger is made up of the words or actions that people use (or do not use) as an expression of their anger feelings. These may range from silent sulking to violent homicide. Some anger expressions are obvious, such as swearing at a person, while others are more subtle, such as gossip, forgetfulness, nicknames, biting humor, talking to oneself, or acting like one does not understand. When the situation or people's own preferences prevent them from expressing their anger openly, they use more of these subtle forms of anger expression.

Tim LaHaye in his book, *Anger Is a Choice*, lists many terms that describe expressions of anger.[19] Differences in the words relate to the degree of anger being felt as well as the specific situation from which the anger has arisen. The list below includes many of LaHaye's terms, but only partially exhausts the many ways we can describe a person's anger expressions.

| | | |
|---|---|---|
| begrudge | sore | huffy |
| loathe | annoyed | furious |
| disdain | resentful | inflamed |
| despise | infuriated | mad |
| abhor | frustrated | irked |
| to kid | exasperated | up tight |
| criticize | irritated | worked up |
| scorn | miffed | griped |
| laugh at | hurt | vexed |
| give someone grief | troubled | crushed |
| cool to | offended | incensed |
| fed up with | sarcastic | grumpy |
| sick of | testy | provoked |
| burned up with | bitter | grouchy |
| cranky | ill tempered | mean |
| touchy | spiteful | cross |
| out of sorts | vicious | jealous |
| savage | enraged | ticked off |
| hot | turned off | disgusted |
| repulsed | moody | indignant |

## THE ANGER MOSAIC

Anger is a surge of autonomic biology, accompanying thoughts, and a chosen pattern of behavior. In every anger situation these three operate at such a smooth, rapid pace that people fail to sense the different components present. Also, since anger is a mosaic of physiological, cognitive, and behavioral states, the nature of anger experiences can vary greatly. While either behaviors or physiological arousal states can affect our counselees' thoughts, their cognitive states normally exercise the greater controlling influence in anger. However, the words people use to describe their angers are almost always feeling or behavioral words. Perhaps this is because in anger, feelings are so vivid and behaviors are so visible that during intense angers the rational component seems to retreat from the scene. People see their angers behaviorally when they describe themselves as being "up in arms," "flying off the handle," "flipping our lid," or "having a conniption fit." Behavioral anger is scowling, snarling, snorting, and sulking. The emotional part of anger dominates our counselees' words, also. They "storm," "boil," or "flare up." They are "hot heads," "hot under the collar," "tinderboxes," "spitfires," "incensed," "inflamed," "fiery," or "combustible" in their emotional fury.

In summary, angers are usually very complex responses as opposed to simple reflexes. As we understand the make-up of the anger response we can come to certain conclusions about anger and its therapy.[20] Since anger contains a physiological, cognitive, and behavioral response, we cannot limit ourselves, as counselors, to observing and working with just the behavioral manifestations of anger. Anger exists inside of people and has to be dealt with there. A distinction needs to be made between arousal feelings of anger and the choices of anger expression people make. Our counselees may feel ashamed of arguing with people, but there is no reason to be ashamed of the natural feelings of anger arousal that they have when they are confronted by another. The mind's involvement in the anger process means that there is hope that the emotion of anger can be controlled or that its energies can be directed along more constructive lines.

## THE POSITIVE SIDE OF ANGER

While anger can grow into hostility and hatred, it does not begin that way. Anger is a feeling of arousal, often an uncomfortable feeling, concerning something that troubles us. As part of our body's natural response system, anger serves us well in several ways. Anger can provide the energy and motivation for certain difficult tasks. Anger, like pain, may also serve as a warning that something is wrong with our attempts to relate to the environment. Finally, anger may benefit our relationships whenever we work through our anger with others.

### Anger's Energy

Since feelings of anger spring from the body's autonomic response system, it can provide the energy and motivation for certain activities. Professional athletes are well aware of the benefits of a "clean" feeling of arousal anger at their opponent. There need not be any sins involved, or hatred or bitterness toward others in this type of anger. Such anger quickens the senses, shoots adrenaline throughout the body, and sends glycogen to fatigued muscles.[21] This feeling of anger can rouse people out of their lethargy or their apathy and get them to attempt difficult tasks or face imposing threats. Anger, therefore, can get people involved with life, especially when it pushes them to stand up against evil and to heal the consequences of evil and suffering. J. L. Moreno called this ethical anger, the type that arises when an individual's value system has been affronted.[22]

The Old Testament gives us many examples of godly, yet angry, men. In Exodus 32, Moses burned with anger at the Hebrew people, when they set up idol worship just as he received the Ten Commandments from God. Moses did not possess all the capabilities to deal with the stubbornness and wickedness of the Hebrew people. But his anger served him well in this case, because, at the height of their shouting and perversity, Moses hurled the tablets of stone to the ground and burned their golden calf in the fire. With the energy of anger he quickly regained control of the Hebrew camp.

In another example, David as a young boy felt anger when he saw the Lord's army stopped in fear of the giant Goliath (1 Samuel 17). This passage does not use the word *anger*, but from David's actions we can infer his emotional response to the situation. His reaction to a pagan giant despoiling God's honor and the Hebrew army cowering in fear gave him the courage to do what his older brothers would not do. We would be in error to think that heroes and heroines are people who feel no fears, and that they casually and without emotion risk their lives for others. The hero feels the same fears as all of us and has to act in spite of fear. David's anger and sense of dependency on God allowed him to act in the face of fear.

At another time David burned with anger as he listened to the prophet Nathan's story about the rich man stealing from the poor man (2 Samuel 12). It may have been this very anger energy that allowed David to respond to Nathan and face the accusation that he was the wicked rich man. David's hot anger seemed to be just what was needed to attack his own pride. He condemned the man in the story and said he deserved to die. When David was told he was that man he (2 Sam. 12:13) readily and humbly admitted his sin.

## Anger's Warning

Physical pain serves the purpose of alerting a person to a problem in the body. Without pain and discomfort people would not remove their hands from hot stoves until it was too late. They would not turn over in bed, until they had bed sores. People would not go to a doctor during an attack of appendicitis, if they could not feel the pain. Anger can also act as a warning that something may be wrong inside of a person. It can be a symptom of deeper disturbances in a personality that need attention. When a wife reacts angrily to her husband's "hello" on the phone, he wants to know what is wrong. When someone uncharacteristically belittles another's work, we know that something else is bothering him. Anger can indicate a growing sense of frustration, a fear of failure, irrational expectations about life, unresolved guilt feelings, or physical exhaustion. Like pain, anger can be an uncomfortable warning to each angry person who needs to ask, why am I being so irritable? Why does that person bother me? Self-examination during times of anger can produce personal growth.

## Anger and Relationships

Expressing anger properly has definite benefits for people and their relationships.[23] At times we get angry with strangers, but more often, anger is directed against loved ones and those with whom we spend time. Anger, therefore, can work for or against relationships. When our counselees learn to handle their anger, they learn to trust themselves to be aroused and still respond appropriately. By expressing anger constructively, our counselees also learn that they can be in control of themselves, even when angry. A positive expression of anger leads people to the conclusion that they sometimes make themselves angry, and they can cease blaming others and harming relationships.

Anger can also be a positive instrument for change and growth in a relationship, when it is controlled by love and an awareness of the other person's rights and worth. Anger expressed between two people can be the first step of mutual love, understanding, and caring in the relationship. Freedom of emotional expression, especially in intimate relationships, allows people to become more honest about the relationship. Anger expressed without malice can lead to helpful changes in relationships, changes that will benefit communication and lead to deeper commitment. People who learn to express their anger properly will gain more respect than those who do not express anger or who express it poorly.[24]

## THE NEGATIVE SIDE OF ANGER

The negative effects of anger are detailed in many places in this book, but a few comments might be helpful here, before we deal with the question of anger and sin. The Bible, without considering all anger to be sin, nevertheless encourages us to refrain from anger. Psalms 37:8 states plainly:

Refrain from anger and turn from wrath;
    do not fret—it leads only to evil.

This passage does not say that anger is evil, but that anger may be the well-worn path to evil. Solomon writes in Ecclesiastes 7:9 that ". . . anger resides in the lap of fools." The book of Proverbs gives us some of the most negative condemnations of anger in the Bible. According to Proverbs, anger causes only trouble. It is related to cruelty (Prov. 27:4) and strife (21:19). As a general rule, anger causes more trouble than good and leads to more sin than righteousness. When people become angry, they are encouraged to let it rise slowly (James 1:19), but to deal with it quickly lest greater harm come to them (Eph. 4:26).

The Bible pictures anger as a dangerous feeling that may not be wrong, but the level of physiological and emotional arousal that people experience during anger can easily cloud their usual rational thinking and remove learned inhibitions to sinful behavior. Angry feelings may be common, but people should learn to deal with them quickly and not allow them to persist. For example, anger feelings often get the best of people when they are driving in heavy traffic. Reacting to crowded highways by honking the horn, swearing, or making obscene gestures is dangerous and does nothing to solve the difficulty of driving in traffic.

## HOSTILITY AND BITTERNESS: WHAT ANGER CAN BECOME

Hostility and bitterness are distinctly different from anger. Anger is a state of arousal in response to troubling situations. By itself anger is a neutral state. It is a natural response that may be expressed constructively or destructively. Hostility and bitterness, in contrast, are not the result of a sudden surge of emotion in response to an unpleasant situation. They are attitudes toward life and people. Hostility and bitterness arise when people hold on to their anger feelings in an unforgiving attitude of resentment. Hostile people are not born that way, but they become progressively more negative about people and events as they fail to deal with their anger constructively. Hostility tends to persist even without cause. In contrast, anger is a temporary situational response.

The word *hostile* comes from the Latin *hostilis,* which means enemy, an appropriate name, since the hostile person is continually at odds with many people and events. The hostile person makes many enemies and has definite hatred for some people. One dictionary defines the word *hostile* with the words "overt antagonism, unfriendly, not hospitable." Hostile people have become embittered and negative through a long series of encounters with life in which they did not deal with their anger. Following each anger episode in their lives, they became resentful as the anger festered. What was originally an emotion of hurt, frustration, or fear became hatred for the offending person or situation.

Pam came to see me concerning her problem with depression and very quickly her bitterness toward her parents became obvious. She did not look angry, but rather, she appeared cold and indifferent and that was how she related to people. Pam's parents had ignored her and made her feel unloved and unwanted for most of her life. She could never do anything to please them, and they treated her as if she was in the way, an expense, a bother, an interruption. Over the years Pam's confusion and hurt turned into bitterness toward her parents and a general distrust of God. With her cold appearance and her caustic personality she held others at arm's length and protected herself from the possible hurt of relationships. When Pam fell in love with a man who loved her as her parents never had, she wanted to end the bitter feelings she had toward her parents and to get on with life and relationships. Counseling did not change Pam's parents' attitudes toward her, but it did allow her to tear down the walls of hostility that she had erected around herself.

Hostility and bitterness grow out of proportion to the negative people or events precipitating them. Hostile people provoke anger and hostility in others and, consequently, they have more reason to increase their own anger and hostility. Hostility is also contagious. A few hostile people create more anger, hostility, and hatred around them and the worst in human beings surfaces. Vengeance satisfies the victor, but the vanquished thirst for vengeance of their own. And, thus, hatred breeds itself.

Human history is a study of hostility, a series of wars, revolutions, murders, and oppressions. We can see the hostility and its effects in the lives of Cain, Esau, Saul and the Pharisees, as well as Atilla the Hun, Adolf Hitler, and others. There are millions of lesser-known hostile people—our modern terrorists and criminals as well as our bitter neighbors and family members.

The negative effects of unrestrained hostility in our world are so extensive that it seems strange that people would need encouragement to abandon hostility and seek peace. But, the formation of hostility from smoldering resentments is a gradual process and there is no one point at which someone decides to become a hostile person. In fact, a hostile, bitter person thinks that his or her hostility is simply a part of the natural human make-up and, thus, cannot be controlled. Among some people, notably terrorists or inner-city gangs, hostility and violence is considered acceptable and even praiseworthy.

However, there is no virtue in hostility and bitterness. It is not right for people to allow resentment to fester as they stubbornly cling to their rights. In normal situations human rights can be protected without violence and hostility. Hebrews 12:14 advises us to "make every effort to live in peace with all men. . . ." Verse 15 goes on to give an explanation as to why we should seek peace, cautioning . . . "that no bitter root grows up to cause trouble and defile many."

Jesus also warned against men being unwilling to give up their angers and refusing to forgive others. Anger that is unwilling to forgive others is not just an emotional arousal, but an attitude of pride that refuses to admit fault. Such an attitude can block one's relationship with God. Unrepentant anger can grow into hostility and hatred. While child abuse, wife abuse, and social violence are not simple problems to solve, they are not diseases or mental illness.[25] They are problems that result from the kind of anger that surfaces to some extent and from time to time in everyone.

## Is Anger a Sin?

It should be clear by now that anger is not wrong when it is defined as the arousal feelings people experience in the presence of threatening or frustrating events. Like all other emotions, anger serves useful purposes in God's design for our lives. Anger, therefore, is ethically neutral, until it is expressed in ways that are inconsistent with scriptural principles. It becomes a sin whenever it is accompanied by wrong thoughts or actions or by motives such as jealousy, envy, selfishness, or conceit.

If anger is a normal human response, then why do certain passages in Scripture clearly teach that it is wrong, for example, Colossians 3:8 and Ephesians 4:31? These passages should be put into the context of Ephesians 4:26, where Paul is not calling anger a sin, but is warning of the possible sins that can come from unresolved anger. The idea that anger is not a sin is supported by passages such as Proverbs 16:32 and James 1:19

which praise the one who is slow to anger. Anger that results in dissension or which is motivated by jealousy or hatred is clearly forbidden by the Bible. Therefore, *it is the sinful expression of anger or the improper motive that turns anger into sin.*

## THE ANGER OF GOD

If the idea of anger without sin seems unbiblical, we must remember that the sin of anger resides in its improper cognitive or behavioral expression. The emotional feeling itself is not sinful. God is described as being angry and expressing it openly (Exod. 32:9, Num. 11:33, Isa. 65:15, Ps. 78:38). Psalms 7:11 says, "God is a righteous judge, a God who expresses his wrath everyday."

The Old Testament has over 450 uses of the word *anger*, approximately 375 of which relate to God's anger. God's anger in the Old Testament seems to be his reaction to human unholiness and ungodliness. Yet, this anger is only one part of God's character. God is also described as being slow to anger (Ps. 103:8, Isa. 48:9, Jon. 4:2, and Nah. 1:3). Therefore, while his wrath is seen as a just response to man's sin, God is also merciful, loving, and compassionate. God's anger is directed by his righteous response to sin, but limited by his patient and merciful character.

In the New Testament we also see Jesus getting angry and expressing it openly. In Mark 3:1–5 he is angry at the Jews' hardened hearts in response to his miracle of healing a man's withered hand. In John 2:13–15 Jesus shows the wrath of God as he drives the moneychangers from the temple. While not every passage covering this story uses the word *anger*, Jesus' anger is a plausible explanation. In this story Jesus is probably angry with the moneychangers who unfairly charge inflated interest rates. His Father's temple was supposed to represent the awesome holiness of God and not the greed of man. Paul is another New Testament example of one who showed anger without sin. He addressed communities angrily when they had to be corrected (Gal. 1:6, 3:1, 4:21, 5:12).

In spite of these and other biblical examples of God's anger without sin, the dominant biblical theme on human anger is that most often in human affairs the expression of anger is wrong. Anger is a natural emotion and has the potential for good, but, since people are fallen beings, it is often a very harmful and damaging emotion. Like Paul, counselors should warn people never to take vengeance (Rom. 12:19), to get rid of all bitterness, rage and anger, and to love each other in a forgiving way (Eph. 4:31–32). Our counselees need to learn to bear with one another and forgive whatever grievances they have against others (Col. 3:13). In this way they can rise above the angers that can so easily beset them.

# CHAPTER THREE

# THE CAUSES OF ANGER

Jan was a college sophomore with an anger problem, but she was mature enough to bring her problem to her pastor. Jan's roommate at college, Dianne, had been anorexic a year earlier and continued to suffer from physical, emotional, and family problems. She began to lose weight and was talking about suicide. Jan was a growing Christian, who looked forward to the opportunity to help her roommate in any way she could. But, as the months wore on Dianne's needs began to drag Jan down. She felt obligated to talk to Dianne whenever the girl was depressed. Jan ate her meals with her instead of with her own friends and included Dianne in her own plans.

Recently, Jan had gone shopping with her friends and had

angrily excluded Dianne. This made Jan feel guilty, because Dianne was talking about suicide again. Jan felt trapped, because she believed her Christian duty was to minister to Dianne without complaint. Yet she felt she was being used. She was giving up her time and plans, but Dianne was getting all the attention and sympathy in the residence hall. Because of this, Jan grew increasingly angry, and, instead of talking to her roommate about how she felt, she began to treat her unkindly. Dianne felt Jan's coldness, and her resulting depression made Jan feel even more guilty about her anger.

The causes of Jan's anger are not simple. But, it is important to get to the causes, because knowing the causes can lead to our methods of therapy. If we think Jan's anger problem was caused by her anorexic roommate, we can suggest that she change roommates. But if we believe that Jan's anger is a product of her own frustrations in college life, we will suggest different solutions.

Like most emotional problems, struggles with anger are not simple. They involve a variety of issues that must be considered by the counselor. These include anger-producing events in the environment, but they also include the individual's own attitudes and freedom to control or master a situation. In the case of Jan, it might be better to speak of the influences on her behavior, or those elements in her life that predispose her to anger.

Four major predisposing influences can affect anger. They are:

1. The body chemistry of the angry person,
2. The environmental circumstances related to the anger situation,
3. The angry person's perception of his or her personal inadequacies or of the social situation, or
4. An underlying character flaw due to one's sin nature.

Human body chemistry is related to how tired or hungry people are, whether they are male or female, and any physical ailments from which they might be suffering. The environmental factors in anger relate to any circumstances immediately affecting one's health, self-perception, or goals. The roommate in our example was the chief environmental element related to Jan's anger. The third influence is the person's own mind-set about life, what one needs to be happy, and his or her feelings of guilt or powerlessness. The fourth area, often not considered in discussions of human emotional problems, is the human condition of fallenness, that is, the inability to meet our own deepest needs, our self-centeredness, and our inability to love self and others.

I have called these four general causes *predispositions and influences*, because I do not want counselors to lose sight of human freedom in the mind's ability to alter its perception of circumstances. Presuppositions are only "pushes" toward anger—sometimes, very strong pushes—and they may seem overpowering. But, it is no help in counseling to make people feel their anger is predetermined by the influences.

We should approach the subject of anger's causes not forgetting what we have already learned about anger. As a biological response, anger develops naturally, even automatically. Look at a young baby. No one has to teach him or her how to get angry. But neither is anyone born hostile and filled with hatred. Anger expression, hostility, and hatred are learned. Children are born with a natural ability to vent their emotions without a second thought. That is why children can be crying one moment as if their hearts are broken, and laughing the next moment without a care. They deal with each feeling simply as it comes. But, as children's social learning and self-perceptions increase, their expressions of anger begin to change. Over time, learning has a greater and greater effect on the anger response, until anger appears to be a rapid, automatic reply to an environmental stimulus.

The answer to the question, what makes people angry? is that *nothing* makes people angry. People make themselves angry. If people are angry, it is because at their most fundamental level they have chosen to be angry. Someone may ask, does it not make you angry when someone criticizes you? The answer to this question I believe is no. My anger may feel like an automatic response to criticism. But in fact, I have learned, probably at an early age, to respond with anger to certain events. I do

45

substantially modify my anger expression when the situation demands more public display of control. Certainly a variety of powerful influences exist around me. However, when I lose my temper, it is because I allow myself to explode along the behavioral patterns dictated by my previous learning.

The !Kung (the *!* represents a click in their language), hunter-gatherers of the Kalahari Desert are often referred to as a people without anger and aggression, but they are no different from everyone else except in their learning and management of anger. They have the same autonomic reactions as other people and internally they are not free from jealousies, resentments, and sulking. The !Kung, however, know that they must manage their emotions lest their nomadic survival be threatened. They have learned to make sharing, not competition, their dominant value.[1]

## THEORIES OF ANGER

There are many scientific theories of why people get angry. Most of them center on uncontrollable biological or psychological urges as opposed to personal, mental involvement in the anger emotion. We will briefly examine three theories: the ethological, biological, and Freudian theories.

### Ethological Theory

Konrad Lorenz set the tone for ethological approaches to anger in his often cited *On Aggression,* in which he saw anger as inborn.[2] Modern ethologists feel that the brain's "primitive" structures, such as the limbic system and hypothalamus, are responsible for the animal-like human emotions of rage, fear, and sexual desire. The fact that humans share these brain structures with lower animals argues, according to ethologists, that human anger has its roots in animal rage. This view tends to give rise to the opinion that people's animal passions are at odds with their reasoning processes.

Charles Darwin gave strong support for this animal view of anger in his theory of evolution. He felt that the origins of all human emotions could be found in the lower animals.[3] Darwin theorized that anger, bitterness, and indignation were only watered-down forms of animal rage, differing only in degree. Human learning and symbolic abilities counted little to Darwin in the production of human anger. Such theories, of course, leave people feeling powerless to control their anger, and anger as a biological reflex becomes morally neutral.

## Biological Theory

Today's biological theories of anger tend to emphasize gene structure, blood chemistry, or brain disease as the causes of anger.[4] The evidences of biological control of animal aggressiveness such as self-defense, maternal aggression, infanticide, and predatory aggression abound in scientific literature. Species-typical behavior, such as frog-killing in rats, appears spontaneously in rats at about age fifty days, and this biological time clock is not altered by the prior experience of the rat. Brain stimulation of the hypothalamus or amygdala of a variety of animals can elicit aggressive behavior. Injection of the hormones testosterone or cortiscosterone in laboratory animals also stimulates aggression.[5] Hormone levels in adolescent boys have been shown to be related to emotional dispositions and aggressiveness.[6] In addition, some successful pharmacological treatments of rage have been reported.[7]

However, there is no evidence to suggest that human aggression is completely controlled by heredity, blood chemistry, or brain disease. It is true that boys' testosterone levels increase with a rise in the frequency of their fighting and aggression.[8] But, teen-age boys have changed social status and their testosterone levels affect their muscles as well as their brains. Therefore, we cannot be sure that the aggression is hormonally produced.

Psychosurgery on the amygdala, hypothalamus, and midbrain areas in humans has produced few positive results in curbing aggression. Neuropsychologist Elliot Valenstein has written excellent critiques of such attempts to correct human aggressive behavior by means of brain stimulation or surgical procedures.[9] In summary, there is no evidence that we will ever discover a gene controlling human hate or selfishness, or that by altering hormone levels or destroying brain tissue we can alter the human passion for war or marital conflict. Biology is involved in all that human beings are as persons, but it does not appear that human anger can be reduced to genetic or biochemical influences alone.

## Freudian Theory

The Freudian approach to anger emphasizes that the human rational, conscious level does not know and cannot control what the irrational, unconscious level is doing in feelings and behavior. Freud, like Darwin, regarded anger as a part of our biological heritage, but Freud more than Darwin saw destruction and violence in human aggression.

Freud's emphasis in explaining human anger and aggression was on the libido with its enormous energy reserves to fuel internal and external battles. If the libido's energy was blocked by social restraints on aggression, the aggressive tendencies would show up elsewhere. This Freudian notion of a huge reservoir of anger energy seeking release later became known as the hydraulic theory. This theory said it was harmful to block the expression of anger, because the pressure of this anger energy would build up to "spill over" or "explode" in violent rage.

Catharsis—the emptying of the emotional reservoirs—became the cure for anger. Cathartic activities, such as talking it out, shouting, exercising, pounding pillows, or plotting revenge became the therapies. These cathartic releases have become known as *emotional ventilation*. In chapter 4 we will look at the inability of unrestrained ventilation of anger to solve anger problems.

All of these theories of anger with their biological roots suggest that anger is a nearly uncontrollable animal passion. Such views are an injustice to both wild and domesticated animals of all species, who live most of their lives without resentment, rage, or violence. An overemphasis on biological or Freudian themes can rob our counselees of the hope that they can change their anger. These theories have a tendency to erase the human moral responsibility for anger actions, which is a first step in solving anger problems. Just because anger begins with biology is no reason to dissolve human responsibility in a vial of adrenaline.

This book will take a position closer to cognitive theories of anger, that anger has a biological component, but that the whole response of anger is generated, shaped, or reduced by how people interpret the world and the events happening to them. For people to be held hostage to their biology and for them to claim that the devil, or DNA made them do it, is not giving credit to their humanness and their responsibility for their emotions. With this emphasis on human responsibility in mind, I will now describe the contributing *influences* in human anger. These are not irreversible causes, but the circumstances within which our angers easily develop. Knowledge of these influences becomes important in counseling, because removing them or working with them can be an important strategy in the counseling of anger.

## THE CONTRIBUTORS TO ANGER

When Peter cut off the ear of Malchus (John 18:10), the servant of the high priest, we could safely say that Peter was angry and aggressive. But Peter's anger or our own is not so simple as to be captured in a word or two. The contributors to Peter's thoughts and feelings on that terrible night and the shapers of his aggressive response must have been many and varied. We can imagine what that night was like.

It was late at night and Peter had gotten very little sleep. An angry mob came upon them suddenly. Peter was terrified, but he felt obligated as one of the leaders of the disciples to do something. Peter loved his master and wished to protect him, but probably he was also angry with Jesus for not avoiding such problems or using his power to destroy his enemies. Peter may have been angry with the other disciples, who were doing nothing to help. His own temperament was volatile, easily moved to laughter, tears, or anger; he was impulsive, and often spoke and behaved without thinking. The mob was pressing in toward him and Jesus. Without thinking, perhaps, Peter swung his sword at an unarmed servant carrying a torch rather than at an armed guard. Peter's fears may have made him swing his sword with half-effort and off-center, and he struck a glancing blow, cutting off the servant's right ear.

The existence of many contributing factors to angry behavior such as Peter's should serve to make us more compassionate when we have to deal with angry people in the counseling office. Without denying that people are responsible for their actions and able to learn to control and modify their anger responses, we need to be patient with angry people. They may be pushed to the brink of anger by circumstances far more demanding than any we have faced. On a hot, humid day, after the air conditioner has failed, the mother of three needs compassion. Anger is close. After several critical remarks have been made to the pastor about his sermon, he needs to be aware that he is close to anger.

I have divided the contributors to anger into two categories, external and internal, to simplify our thinking about them. External contributors hammer on a person from the outside and are considered external even though they may become a part of one's mind-set. Internal contributors originate inside the person, are strongly affected by the external contributors, and are generally related to views of self.

## EXTERNAL CONTRIBUTORS TO ANGER

### Childhood Learning

Children learn about expressing their anger from their parents' styles of anger expression and from the family's acceptable outlets for anger. Very early, children are influenced by the conflicts between their parents.[10] Children are often taught to stifle their anger, especially anger at their parents or siblings. Parents often threaten punishment when they see their children's anger or disrespect. A comprehensive longitudinal study carried out in New York state on grade-school children revealed that certain qualities of children's experiences at home—particularly their parents' behaviors—were associated with aggressiveness in the children.[11]

What children need is an open-home environment, where they can learn how to express the anger going on inside of them. The inability to express anger properly as an adult may be related to improper learning as children. The importance of this early learning could be the impetus behind Paul's warning in Ephesians 6:4 to not discipline children in ways that provoke them to anger. Counselors should advise parents that in order to reduce their children's aggressiveness they need first to reduce their own aggressiveness toward their children, and then work to change their children's perceptions of those people or events that frustrate them.

## Christian Teaching

Another hindrance to the proper expression of anger may be mistaken ideas about Christianity and anger.[12] The biblical view of anger is often erroneously taught in this manner: Do not express your anger. All anger is a sin. Be ashamed of your feelings. Do not be assertive for your rights.

An incorrect understanding of the Christian view of anger can lead people to deny that they are angry or to suppress it, only to have their anger show up in more subtle behaviors. For this reason much of the anger that counselors must deal with is of the passive-aggressive type, anger that is expressed more subtly than shouting and arguing.

## Work

Certain occupations can make people more vulnerable to feelings of anger.[13] This is because a job can present a great number of opportunities for stress, disappointment, and frustration, and yet, the environment may not allow for anger expression. The pastor's job is a perfect example of this double bind. The pastor has more reasons to be angry than most (low pay, long hours, endless demands) and a work environment that frowns on anger expression, particularly in Christian leaders. The pastor is expected to minister to everyone's needs and listen to all complaints, and yet he or she has little control over major decisions.

The house-bound mother has a similar anger-causing job, with high demands, no pay, and many irritations. Her anger is affected by the presence and age of children in the home, her involvement (or lack of it) in decision-making, her contact with friends, and her husband's educational level.[14] She sometimes has no one to whom to express her frustrations except her husband, who asks her how her day went but wants no more than a two-sentence answer.

Working mothers also show high amounts of anger and

hostility. Women who report placing careers ahead of family score higher than other women in anxiety, depression, and hostility.[15] Power struggles and intergroup competition are also responsible for on-the-job anger and hostility.[16] The stresses of promotions, pecking orders, and job security also correlate to the increase of anger in the home.[17]

## Competition and Sports

Competition, whether in school, sports, business, or in people simply comparing themselves with others, puts stress on one's sense of self-worth.[18] Winning or getting ahead contributes to self-worth, while losing stirs up feelings of insecurity and inferiority.

The amount of hostility people express can usually be correlated with their sense of self-worth at the time and how they feel they "measure up." It is always easier for one to be kind and gracious after winning a race or getting a promotion, than after one fails. Sports, exercise, and tense competition of any type generate increased levels of adrenaline hormones and make people more susceptible to feeling intense emotions.[19] Since all anger feelings begin with the body's arousal system, a body that is aroused is already halfway to an emotion like anger. The ones who become angry are those who are both aroused and provoked.[20] Anger following a near accident in an automobile is a similar phenomenon, because the driver is aroused by the emergency and may be provoked by the other driver. Laboratory-designed competitive tasks with built-in failure rates are also reliable producers of anger and aggression in experimental subjects.[21]

People may lessen their anger episodes in competitive sports if they are aware that their arousal feelings stem from physical exertion. They should not readily label these feelings "anger." Experiments have shown that people in good physical condition, for whom the arousal of exercise drops off rapidly, are less likely to mistake exercise arousal for anger arousal after a six-minute recovery period.[22] The individual must also be aware that trying to release anger energy through contact sports does not always work.[23] As in marital conflicts, when anger is encouraged, more, not less, anger occurs.[24]

## Noise and Crowds

Noise and crowds, like sports, do not instinctually release anger in people. Instead, they generate physical arousal, which can become coupled with provocation or fear. For some people, who are on vacation or are visiting a parade in the city, the arousal feelings in a crowd can bring forth feelings of exhilaration. Whether or not people get angry in the presence of loud noises depends upon what the noises represent to them.[25]

Loud noises do produce an increase in adrenaline. But anger at a baby's cry or a radio's loud blasting only results if such is interpreted by the person as being harmful or frustrating to him.[26] If the cause of noise is a benefit to people, then those people are less likely to be angry. The same is true for crowds and traffic. Anger depends on whether a crowd is seen as a threat, a trap, or making one late.

Driving a car in traffic is particularly arousing, because the task demands constant attention and split-second reactions. Therefore, anger is a constant passenger in traffic jams. In order to be able to control their anger, drivers need to know when arousal-producing situations are going to occur, and then prepare themselves mentally to avoid or counter anger interpretations.

## Physical Health

The constant presence of pain, weariness, and the poorly-understood biochemical changes in hypoglycemia or premenstrual syndrome are frequent contributors to anger.[27] When drug therapies are used to relieve depression, hostility in patients decreases as well and a friendlier mood is often reported.[28] As with arousal in sports or crowds, if people realize that their feelings are potentially a product of their bodily states and not necessarily related to their companions, they can lessen their tendencies to anger. Also, helping counselees realize that they are prone to anger at certain times can help them prepare for the stress involved.

## Alcohol

Social drinking seems to produce an ambiguous change of mood, which can contribute to a variety of feelings, including anger. Whether or not people get angry under the influence of alcohol depends in part upon what they believe alcohol does to them and what social environment they are in. Alcohol acts initially as a stimulant, which perks a person up and increases heart rate. Larger amounts of alcohol than one or two drinks begin to act on the body as a depressant, which is first seen in drowsiness, slurred speech, and difficulty in walking.

The connection between alcohol and anger may be more of a social link than a physiological one.[29] Alcohol may make it difficult to drive a car or to rationally express thoughts, but it does not loosen the learned, social reins that control behaviors. People who grow angry when they drink may expect this effect from alcohol or they may be using alcohol as an excuse to vent their feelings. Alcohol has probably been a convenient excuse for thousands of years to do foolish and sinful things that people would not ordinarily do. The dominant effect of alcohol is to depress mood and to slow bodily responses, not to get people into verbal exchanges and fist fights. The best thing to do for people who get violently angry when drinking, is to hold them morally and legally accountable for their anger.

## INTERNAL CONTRIBUTIONS TO ANGER

### Self-Esteem and Self-Sufficiency Needs

The more people have self-image problems, the more self-absorbed their lives tend to become. They become keenly and painfully aware of daily events and how those events affect them. To people with low self-esteem, ordinary situations can become threatening; fears, hurts, and jealousies rise easily to the surface.[30] Anger is never far behind. In experimental situations anger has been found to be more easily produced in subjects by threatening their self-esteem than by other methods.[31] Feeling lonely, defeated, or inadequate in life may lead to the need to be first, best, most important, and the constant need to pursue feelings of importance.[32] People become angry in such circumstances, because they are constantly feeling their importance threatened. When they are criticized in areas where they feel strong and talented, people are less likely to get angry than when they are criticized in areas of perceived weaknesses, which criticism they have trouble accepting. Videotape studies show laughter often has the ability to dispel anger because laughter at self or a situation can eliminate shame, allowing anger to dissipate.[33]

A degree of self-sufficiency is good for a person's self-image, since it contributes to independence and motivation for many tasks in life. But the striving for complete self-sufficiency and independence negatively affects the mutual sharing of close relationships. People who try to be self-sufficient are easily frustrated and angered by evidence of their dependence on others. They get angry at themselves for needing others and angry at others for "keeping" them in this weakness.

## The Desire for Power in Relationships

Power in a relationship is feeling in control of one's own behavior. Of course, the essence of a good relationship is fitting one's behavior into the life of another, and, thus, the surrender of some power. The surrender of power in a love relationship should be nonthreatening. People who feel threatened in relationships often use anger to restore to themselves power or control over what happens. This seems to be the reason why male batterers are more likely to be rated as lower in masculinity than nonviolent husbands.[34] Anger supports a batterer's quest for power by intimidating others and cautioning them in the use of their own power. People start tiptoeing around angry people, never troubling them, asking for their cooperation, or confronting them. Rousing their anger is too expensive a price to pay. Racial hostilities reflect, in part, a reaction to power or loss of power to another group in the ongoing struggle for status and advantage.[35]

## The Desire to Be Perfect

Related to self-esteem and self-sufficiency needs and the desire for self-sufficiency and power is the desire to be perfect. Perfectionism results in anger, whenever there is a loss of imagined perfection. The perfectionist may be very talented, but still sets up unrealistic standards, which must be met in order to feel fully worthwhile and accepted. The A student gets angry and depressed over a B+. The golfer becomes furious at a hooked drive. The homemaker becomes irritated because of dust on the furniture.

Perfectionists tend to get irritated and angry when people or situations block their goals. They also set high standards for others to reach, and are quick to get angry and become judgmental. They are also easily hurt by others who do not treat them with the same perfect concern that they may set as a goal for themselves.

The perfectionist who is a Christian faces some additional problems.[36] Christian growth for these people is slow, because they have difficulty admitting to their inadequacies and faults. They are afraid that their imperfections are repulsive to God and others around them. Therefore, they live a lie that they are really as good as they imagine themselves to be. But they will find more love and acceptance from others and the spiritual resources for Christian growth, when they accept who they really are and give up the myth of perfection.

Perfectionists may even be chronic confessors, but such activity has only the appearance of real honesty in regard to their limitations. Perfectionists are easily angered, because they want to believe that they are always right, and that issues are black and white. Their opinions are strong and rational disagreement with them is difficult.

There is something of the perfectionist in most of us. We vacillate between laziness and perfectionist striving. Many of us consider average and mediocre to be failure. We set unrealistic expectations on ourselves and the world around us. We expect to lose weight every day, and we expect our cars to never fail.

People often despair in themselves because they see so many talented, successful people in the mass media. But, they need to accept their limitations, to accomplish whatever is realistically within their grasp, to realize that maturing is a process of growth from where they are to something better, and to see events and situations in which they fail as only a tiny portion of life. Counselors need to remind people to forget "perfect" marriages and families and jobs, and accept people for what they are, and at the same time continue to strive for the growth that leads to maturity.

## Frustration

A common contributor to anger in a variety of circumstances is the feeling of frustration, which results when people are blocked from acquiring what they pursue. Anger at flat tires may be frustration anger if a person feels he or she is going to be late for an important engagement. People may become frustrated and angry when they cannot finish their work on time. Mothers sense frustration when their care for sick children leaves them no time to do the laundry. In American culture, people are frustrated and angered by interruptions and by time delays, by long lines and short notices. A sense of frustration does not directly cause anger, but like most contributors, it will be interpreted in ways that either do or do not lead to anger.

How much frustration people experience will depend upon the importance of their goals, the duration of the frustrating event, and whether they anticipated the frustrations.[37] Minor frustrations that catch us by surprise usually cause anger, but waiting in a long line for an excellent movie may be seen as well worth the trouble. High taxes or gas rationing during wartime creates less anger-causing frustrations than when there is no enemy to fight. In addition, violent outbursts from individuals who are rarely violent often happen after lengthy periods of continual frustration.[38]

## Guilt Feelings

Unresolved guilt feelings about their failures leave our counselees touchy and irritable about these areas. A wife, who is accused by her husband of flirting with another man, is more likely to get angry if she feels guilty about her thoughts and behavior. The reason for this type of anger, which fights against an accusation, is that people have trouble fully admitting faults to themselves; they are inwardly defending themselves. When people admit faults and know their weaknesses, there is no need for their internal defenses to lash back in anger. People who know they are innocent or who feel repentant for doing wrong are less likely to become angry at accusations, since they no longer have to defend themselves. Unfortunately, much behavior cannot always be clearly labeled right or wrong, and there are extenuating circumstances and gray areas in behavior. Therefore, during confrontations and accusations, a lot of anger is usually present.

### Rejection, Threat, or Hurt

To be rejected by others' words or actions leaves people feeling hurt and worthless. Self-concept comes largely from our perceptions of others' opinions of and love for us. When we feel that others—particularly significant others—disdain our contributions or consider us inferior and unimportant, we tend to bolster self from within by rejecting others. The primary weapons of this rejection are anger and hostility.

This type of anger happens when people feel criticized, humiliated, or "put down," especially in front of others. When they are threatened by a person's accusations and by physical threats, the feelings they have of vulnerability and weakness lead to anger which makes self feel stronger. Hurt people often respond in anger, either with hostile behavior or inner resentment. Individuals described as high-anger subjects score lower on socialization—in areas such as the desire to get along and make good impressions—than do subjects who are described as low-anger individuals.[39]

While this anger of rejection may temporarily make people feel better or protect them from the attacks of others, it does not help to heal relationships. Anger follows hurt so rapidly that people often do not have time to tell their offenders that they (the offenders) are hurting them. To tell a man or woman that he or she is causing hurt very often softens the attacks and threats, and makes for more productive communication. Anger in response to hurt tends to cycle back as more threats and anger.

If husbands and wives, who have just been hurt by the unkind words of their spouses, would immediately say, "I am really hurt by what you said," the mood of the relationship would generally soften. When a man attacks his spouse who has hurt him, cross words quickly escalate. Innocent situations and arguments suddenly burn out of control. Such escalation of harsh words in marriage is the reason that couples find themselves arguing over the tiniest of things.

## Perceptions of Situations

How we interpret stressful events or attacks by others is very important in determining whether we will react in anger or not.[40] Our mind-set, our expectations, and our views of life and immediate events have strong effects on our feelings of anger. This is why giving good excuses will often lessen people's anger.[41] And people who are habitually aggressive are likely to attribute their misfortunes to the hostile behavior of others.[42] This attribution of hostile intent is also characteristic of alcoholics, even after treatment programs for alcoholism.[43]

A different outlook is the reason why something that does not bother me will cause another person to rage. For example, when I went to buy a tire for our car, my wife and I reacted quite differently to the discovery that we also needed new brakes on all the wheels. JoAnn and I had agreed that, though we were short on money, we needed the tire. But when I called JoAnn and told her that what was going to cost $70 was now going to cost $270, she was disheartened and angry about the situation. My response had been more matter of fact; I was looking at the bad brakes, and already anticipating the security of driving a car that was in good shape. The safety was worth the cost to me. To JoAnn, on the other hand, spending money on greasy auto parts did not seem to be worth the same money spent on children's clothes or other pressing household expenses. Anger is formed in the mind, not in bad brakes or under hot collars.

### THE BIBLE AND THE ROOTS OF ANGER

It is often easy for the counselor to see that counselee angers are related to flat tires, hot days, noisy kids, and unkind remarks. But, why is it that people are so susceptible to anger, such that it characterizes their daily lives? This question demands a deeper look at human personality.

## Sin Nature and Self-Centeredness

The Bible describes the historic Fall of Adam and Eve as an original disobedience that crippled human nature. Adam and Eve's disobedience caused spiritual, mental, and physical consequences in their natures, which consequences were inherited

59

by every human being. These effects were first, spiritual death, which means alienation from God and the inability to meet the deepest needs in life. Fallenness also means that Adam and Eve became self-centered beings; that is, they experienced reality from the center of their own existence. This independence from God is characterized by an idiom in Genesis 3; after the original sin, Adam and Eve's "eyes became opened" and . . . they became like God (Gen. 3:7, 22). This self-centered state of mind meant that self-needs and self-perceptions became the filter through which all events were perceived.

Immediately after their sin we see Adam and Eve, who are reacting from self-centeredness, run and hide from God, and blame others. They also are ashamed of their appearance. The results of this new self-centered state of existence were fear, weak self-images, and pride, which became the backbone to problems of anger and hostility. The human inability to meet the deepest needs of life, combined with fear, a poor self-image, and pride, make people insecure when encountering the irritations and trials of life. And that leaves them easily offended and reluctant to forgive. Fallenness also means that they inherit dying bodies and live in a world that suffers under a physical curse. Physical weaknesses contribute to anger's possibilities; when people face irritations, discomforts, pains, and death, they are often angry.

### Anger from Our Sin Nature

Bert Ghezzi in *The Angry Christian* discusses roots of anger that relate directly to our sin nature.[44] He sees two of the primary causes of anger to be holding on to things and resentment. When we grasp things that should be yielded to God, and then lose those things, we are angered.

This holding on can be our attempts to possess material security, success, or our hopes of keeping things unchanged in life. But in this life, all things change and nothing lasts forever. All of us must eventually lose everything we have, including our successes and health as we age and die. One character in C. S. Lewis's *The Great Divorce* is angry at the death of her son, even angry enough to stay in hell.[45] Her rights and her anger were at the center of her mind instead of God.

Resentment, the holding of a grudge against someone or something, is the root of many angers. Resentment comes with pride and the valuing of oneself over others. An unwillingness to forgive others relates directly to a view that says "I am better" or "I would never do such a thing." Honest recognition of one's own faults makes it easier to look at others' faults with compassion. The pride and self-righteousness of our sin nature, however, lead to resentment and hostility.

As human beings, we were created for much more than we can ever experience in our fallen condition. We have deep desires to develop to our fullest potential, but the limitations imposed on us by the consequences of the sin nature and a fallen world frustrate these desires. The deep longing for love in many relationships, the aspiration to develop talents to the fullest, and to be secure and happy in life are testimonies to that for which God created people. Human beings are a dynamic, active species with interests and drives that go far beyond their own abilities to satisfy them.

This desire for fulfillment is continually thwarted by our fallen natures, with the result that we are frustrated and angry.

In this chapter, we have seen that counselors should understand that anger is a complex emotional response. It is tied up with everything we human beings are as persons. The anger we experience begins with bodily arousal systems, but the occasions and strength of that arousal will vary because of physical factors, all the way from our personal brain chemistry to whether we have just eaten or not. This raw, emotional state becomes anger only when the mind gives meaning and context to what we are feeling. Anger is shaped by our mental state, along with our expectations, hopes, fears, and philosophical beliefs about life. Beliefs about life's purpose and the meaning of suffering, views of one's own importance, and one's sense of responsibility and morality all create our potential for anger and the nature of our chosen anger response. With time and repetition, anger responses become ingrained and habitual, and though anger resides in the will, it feels beyond control.

# CHAPTER FOUR

## HOW NOT TO DEAL WITH ANGER

Jane and George are wife and husband. Jane is the expressive partner in the marriage. Outgoing, friendly, and assertive, she is quick to express her opinions and her dissatisfactions about people or events in her life. Jane is also prone to sudden bursts of angry words and, in some cases, loud shouting and door slamming.

Her husband George is the opposite of his wife in many ways. A calm person with steady emotions, he is conscious of his image in public and, therefore, he strives to be in control of himself and his feelings. He seeks to avoid confrontations because he finds the feelings they raise in himself too uncomfortable. George rarely expresses his anger or disappointment in public, but occasionally loses his temper with his children.

In arguments with his wife, George seeks to remain calm and in control. He is afraid that displays of his own anger will further inflame his wife, making a bad situation worse. He tries to control himself in arguments with Jane, because her anger is a picture to him of what he does not want to be, visibly enraged and out of control. But George is angry inside. His anger remains unexpressed. He argues his case mentally after the main event, even muttering swear words, when his wife has stormed out of the room.

George and Jane illustrate two basic ways people tend to handle their anger feelings—rage and resentment—ways that have very few benefits. These styles spring, in part, from a person's own temperament and also as learned habits of anger response. Rage is the act of giving in to our feelings of anger and blowing up, usually verbally, although rage may also be manifest as swearing, screaming, criticizing, condemning, name-calling, or throwing tantrums.

Resentment is the act of holding anger feelings inside. It is usually characterized by angry thoughts or unkind, unfriendly feelings in the presence of another. George, in the above example, may be slower to realize his problem than Jane, whose problem is on public display. In fact, Jane feels very guilty and ashamed of her anger at her family, and she wants to change and improve her relationships. George, on the other hand, often feels self-righteous and believes that he is the injured party, since he did not "lose his cool." His inner resentments and bitterness are much more harmful than his wife's displays of anger, since he fails to recognize or deal with his problem.

Both of these styles of anger expression can be harmful and sinful, because they destroy human relationships. Both George and Jane are controlled by their feelings and neither is free to act in consciously thoughtful ways that seek to resolve problems and build relationships. In the improper expressions of anger that I have just illustrated, both rage and resentment are sins of selfishness, because they serve self-interests rather than the relationship's needs.

Very few people exhibit only one of these two styles of anger expression. George may favor harboring his bitterness and resentment, but he has his temper outbursts also, particularly if he gets drawn into a verbal exchange with his wife. His rage shows up in other situations, such as anger at his children or outward signs of anger when he is alone. Jane may openly vent her anger on George, but she quickly sees how ineffective that is. She becomes ashamed of her temper and, therefore, she leaves the room or the house in her fury. Then she begins to hold her anger in with resentment. Since her visible anger produced no communication, only hard feelings, and solved none of the original grievances, Jane feels worse than before. Her resentment dominates her thinking, until she cools down or until the next angry outburst.

## RESENTMENT: BURYING ANGER

The suppression of anger feelings and the resulting resentment is perhaps the most common response to feelings of anger. Many common expressions well define this behavior. People "bury" their anger, "stuff" it, "sit" on it, "swallow" it, "can" it, and "bottle" it. We clam up and put a lid on it. This style of suppressing anger has been variously labeled as nonassertiveness,[1] somatizing,[2] and the nice-lady syndrome.[3]

Anger feelings that are buried can result in transference, which is misplaced anger. The anger is held in temporarily and then redirected away from the initial cause of anger toward some other person or thing. When a man cannot express his anger toward his boss or his job, he may easily bring it home and express it toward his children and the mess they made in the garage.

Buried anger does not always remain a conscious anger, because people may camouflage their angers with rationalization or self-righteous thoughts. By calling their feelings "righteous indignation," or by too easily excusing another person's unkind behavior toward them, many people are able to convince themselves that they are not angry. Resentment, bitterness, and even hatred can continue unrecognized and undealt with for years, because of such camouflaging.

## Passive-Aggression

Buried anger can also be expressed in ways known as passive-aggression, in which behavior is characterized by both passivity and aggression. The latter is typically expressed by procrastination, obstructionism, stubbornness, or intentional inefficiency. Passive-aggressive behavior often reflects anger that a person would not dare express openly. A passive-aggressive husband avoids helping his wife, when he sees her struggling with several tasks or with their kids. His aggression is a subtle way of retaliating without being fully conscious of the hostile motives involved. His actions are a way of saying: "You deserve this trouble for what you have done to me." Married couples may also use low sexual responsiveness as a form of anger expression.

Parents are especially prone to use passive-aggressive anger with their children. A parent's temper outburst with a child usually does not hurt. In fact, an older child tends to tune this out. To get even, parents will often poke fun at a child, knowing that it hurts the child's feelings. An angry parent throws the baseball too hard, or becomes needlessly picky about a messy room or an early bed time. The effect of this type of passive-aggression is to belittle the child or to make him or her angry. This is unfair to children, because they are still learning how to control their feelings. It will also backfire, because children soon learn ways of raising a parent's ire. This unfair treatment of children may be the reason the Bible warns against embittering children for the purpose of getting even, or for asserting parental superiority (Col. 3:21).

The one person in a group who is always the obstructionist, always against everything, or who makes simple things difficult or short meetings long is demonstrating passive-aggressive anger. Other passive-aggressive styles include being chronically tardy, purposely playing dumb when someone is giving instructions, or performing sluggishly or sloppily on the job while smiling at the boss and pretending to cooperate.

I recall watching a seven-year-old Little Leaguer immediately slow up his run for second base when he heard his dad yell, "Move! Get the lead out!" Some people become sloppy about their appearance when they know it bothers others. Some people dress in ways that displease their spouses, or they remain unconcerned about weight gain or a nagging cough. "If you are for it, then I'm against it," seems to be the attitude.

Teen-agers make good use of this style of anger when they adopt the latest rages in dress and speech. If blue hair and no bra bother mom and dad, great! Parents would be well-advised to learn some discernment into the motives behind their teen's behaviors.

Passive-aggression also comes disguised as humor. While it probably is not valid to conclude that all humor is aggressive, it is at least clear that much sarcasm and sexist slander, and many ethnic slurs, are hostile in nature. Humorous insults and criticism serve anger by lifting the aggressive person up at another's expense. Children and teen-agers are particularly fond of using nicknames that ridicule and diminish people. Though the abused teen may laugh, no one likes to be called "Turkey," "Dingbat," "Chubs," or "Pizza Face." This humor may be relatively harmless as anger goes, but it certainly does not affirm people or demonstrate obedience to Ephesians 4:29, which instructs us to let no unwholesome words pass through our lips.

The suppression of anger and its many forms of passive-aggressive or disguised hostility may be so common because temper outbursts are looked down upon. Most people are ashamed of losing their tempers in public, and a loss of rational control in any emotion may be perceived as a weakness. Anger flare-ups can also get people into trouble, since they invite anger in return. People are usually very careful about becoming angry around their bosses, neighbors, and policemen. Most often spouses, children, waitresses, or passing motorists, are the recipients of overt hostilities.

Christians often suppress anger because they believe that the feelings of anger are sinful. Biblical passages such as Galatians 5:20, Colossians 3:8, and Ephesians 4:31 have been used to teach that anger is sinful and one should not express it. This fails to recognize that the Bible teaches legitimate expressions of anger, such as that of Jesus with the moneychangers in the temple. Sin may also spring up or multiply, because anger feelings have been suppressed and not dealt with. The angry thoughts that rehearse what one should have said in an argument are more likely to be sinful than the honest expressions of hurt and disappointment during the argument.

Pastors, who are to model Christian maturity, and women, who may be restrained by teachings on submission, often see overt expressions of anger as wrong. It would be enlightening, indeed, to compare the church image and the home image of church attenders and see the radical transformation of sweet expressions of peace at eleven o'clock on Sunday morning into signs of normal anger on Sunday afternoon. Suppressed anger is not Christian peace. The anger is there and it is not being dealt with.

### Problems with the Suppression of Anger

Holding anger in and allowing some time to pass is often helpful in learning how to express anger properly.[4] Problems arise, however, with the suppression of anger feelings. Those problems concern the damage that buried anger inflicts on one's emotional peace and relationships.

A popular theory of anger, sometimes labeled the hydraulic theory, compares anger to steam under pressure. Unless the pressure is drained off through the venting of anger, says the theory, the pressure will continue to build up inside people to their own hurt. The hydraulic theory of anger is difficult to accept because repressed anger does not exist as so much quantifiable energy that can be stored. When people speak of anger "building up," they more correctly mean that they have experienced a progressive series of irritations, rejections, or losses of power, and they continue to dwell on these and refuse to let their resentments go. The build-up of one angry feeling and thought after another is draining on the body and mind and cannot be endured by most people without the development of some physiological pathology and some psychological stress. Every time such people think about the anger-producing situation, they feel hurt and angry all over again, and the stress continues long after the provoking events.

It is not clear that buried anger directly causes ulcers, migraines, colitis, and high blood pressure. In relating anger to psychosomatic illness, it seems reasonable to say that anger must take its place as a cause of disease only as a part of a long list of contributing factors.[5] However, a growing amount of evidence suggests that suppressed anger does relate to hypertension and heart disease. Hypertensives, who are quick to respond physiologically to stress, show high amounts of suppressed anger.[6] Findings also confirm a link between aggressive behaviors and painful muscle tension.[7] In the case of heart disease, suppressed hostility is also an implicated factor.[8] Logan Wright, in his presidential address to the American Psychological Association in 1987, warned that for coronary risk based on type-A factors, suppressed anger has proved to be the key ingredient.[9]

Suppressed anger can also give rise to increased worry and anxiety because of people's doubts about their abilities to control themselves, and their fears for relationships or for the consequences of their angers. Those who suppress anger usually develop guilt feelings, because they believe that their anger is wrong. Yet they may face inner tensions because they believe someone has wronged them. Anger thoughts can consume their mental lives and prohibit them from thinking and planning joyfully and constructively about their lives and their jobs.

## The Sin of Resentment

The British poet William Blake wrote of the negative consequences of suppressed anger in his poem, "The Poison Tree." In it we can see a useful distinction between not expressing our anger, because of polite restraint, and suppressing it while harboring resentment and hatred within.

I was angry with my friend;
I told my wrath, my wrath did end.
I was angry with my foe;
I told it not, my wrath did grow.

And I watered it in fears,
Night and morning with my tears,
And I sunned it with smiles
And with soft deceitful wiles.

And it grew both day and night,
Till it bore an apple bright,
And my foe beheld it shine,
And he knew that it was mine—

And into my garden stole
When the night had veiled the pole:
In the morning, glad, I see
My foe outstretched beneath the tree.[10]

"The Poison Tree" is a good description of resentment—anger that people hold in, refuse to give up, nurse along, and hide from a convicting world until it is growing inside their heads like huge poison trees. And their foes remain their enemies until death.

In resentment, the anger is held in and not dealt with; it is only allowed to increase. The enemy is slaughtered and the hostility is relished in the safe privacy of the mind. In Blake's poem the anger ends when people work through it with their friends. But anger grows when people hold it inside and purpose to keep it strong. Blake writes that his inner fears and anguish stimulated his anger to grow. In the presence of the enemy he faked a smile and spoke politely—but the lie and deceit concealed growing anger. Eventually he rejoiced in the downfall of his foe.

## RAGE: VENTILATING ANGER

The other common method of handling anger feelings is to express them openly and vigorously. This may mean confronting offensive people, letting someone know when he or she is wrong, cursing at every irritation, or vocally expressing displeasure at disappointing events. This method of expressing anger feelings has been variously labeled "blowing up," "blowing our top," "flipping one's lid," being "bent out of shape," or "steamed," and "letting it fly." This expression of anger feelings can range from ordinary loss of temper to a violent act of murder. Approval for ventilating anger as opposed to suppressing it has, in part, come from biological theories of anger which see animal aggressiveness as the prime source of human emotions and from the hydraulic theory, which stresses the need to release anger to prevent a dangerous build-up of the anger energy.[11]

### Anger Hurts People

The primary reason that improper anger expression is frowned on by polite society and is generally considered a sin in the Bible is that it hurts others. The door-slamming, fist-shaking, voice-raising style of anger expression may feel good to many people, but they must also consider those on the receiving end of this rage. It is not the outwardness of the anger or the severity of it that makes these expressions wrong. Anger feelings are normal and not sinful. These anger expressions are wrong because they are usually directed at hurting others or are allowed to get out of control, whether someone is hurt or not.

Undisciplined and thoughtless anger explosions do not solve problems between people; but they usually serve to intensify the hostile feelings. Although I need to express my feelings to others, to lash out in a hostile manner whenever I feel like it is not the appropriate method.

Uncontrolled anger and rage touch off a chain reaction in which a person's anger produces anger in others. Not only do people embarrass themselves by being out of control, but their harsh treatment of and lack of consideration for others creates resentment and invites retaliation in kind. The anger problem grows rather than disappears.[12] What usually begins as an unkind remark can lead to a sharp exchange of words and even physical violence, all out of proportion to the original source of dissatisfaction. Anger grows in this chain reaction until people hear themselves saying things they do not mean or never meant to bring up. In the middle of their temper explosions they quickly lose control. An argument begins in a bar over an athletic team and one man is shot. Two men get into a fistfight over a taxi. A wife stabs her husband in an argument that began over how to spell a word. The impetus of biblical passages such as Romans 12:17, "do not repay anyone evil for evil," or Matthew 5:39, ". . . do not resist the evil person," or Proverbs 15:18, "a hot-tempered man stirs up dissension, but a patient man calms a quarrel"—all make this point.

Conflict, especially verbal hostility, keeps problems going and leads to more conflict, but shouting and storming usually do not accomplish anything productive.[13] Hostility puts other people on the defensive and they become unable or unwilling to listen to an angry person's case or plea. Children and many adults tend to respond to the visibly angry person by turning off their "hearing aids" and ignoring them. The ten-year-old child, at whom his mother is screaming, is thinking, *there she goes again.* Nothing Mom is saying sinks in. In his anger at his children a father keeps shouting at them, "Are you listening to me?" Or he shouts the same things over and over because he knows the kids are not listening, and this makes parents all the angrier.

Harriet Lerner in her book *The Dance of Anger* writes that angry women are particularly vulnerable to fulfilling society's stereotype of a nagging, complaining, bitchy woman.[14] When the angry woman is loud and out of control, she is allowing others to write her off as saying nothing of importance; she is not to be taken seriously. A clear, controlled, thoughtful expression of anger is a much more valuable tool for homemakers and businesswomen who want to be listened to.

One negative effect of a hostile expression of anger is that enraged people can force others to change, but not for the right reasons. Tantrums frighten people and many will do whatever they can to get an angry person to calm down. They may obey, cease complaining, or stay out of the way, but not because they appreciate the angry person's feelings. Instead of gaining more respect from people, enraged people usually get less; no one dares bother them, but no one cares for them either.

Behaving aggressively and out of control does not drain a person of hostilities, but actually lowers the individual's inhibitions against anger and he or she becomes angrier than before.[15] Research supports what should be our ordinary experience that aggression is not the catharsis for anger.[16]

It is also worth asking whether the venting of angry feelings, with another person or a counselor, helps the person. Research suggests that the *way* we choose to vent our angry feelings with another determines whether our hostilities will be lessened.[17] If counselees gripe about their problems or the persons with whom they are angry, the act of reciting their complaints builds up emotional arousal, making them angry all over again. Counselors need to be very careful in instructing clients in how to express their anger in a counseling session if the clients are expected to control their anger outside the counseling office. Sharing anger with a friend or a counselor is helpful, if the motive is to gain insight into the feelings and the exact cause of the anger.

### The Anger Trap: Is There Any Way Out?

It appears as if our counselees are stuck between the proverbial rock and a hard place with their anger. When their natural feelings of anger and irritations arise, our counselees seem to have the unenviable choice of either grinning and bearing it or shouting and screaming it. Either way can harm their relationships with others. In daily living, a person does not exclusively choose one of these styles of anger expression; the angry individual uses both. He or she vacillates between holding in the irritations, when the penalties are too great for a shouting match, and letting it all go, when surprised by a provoking situation. What style of anger expression one uses does not matter because both styles serve the same self-centered goals and produce similar negative results. Anger of either style protects self and attacks others. This is the anger trap.

Counselors have to realize that the way out of the anger trap for the counselee is not to erase these two forms of anger expression from the individual's behavior, but to change them. Instead of holding anger *in*, a person should hold it *back* and deal with the anger internally. And, instead of letting anger explode and harm relationships, he or she can learn to work with anger internally. A person can also learn to express anger properly and in ways that respect people and solve problems. To work with anger feelings internally and to express anger properly are the subjects of the next two chapters and the best ways to counsel angry and hostile people.

# CHAPTER FIVE

## SLOW TO ANGER: HOLDING ANGER BACK

"My husband is always screaming at me and the kids! I'm afraid he's going to hurt us." Mary Glass began to cry as she continued to talk about her husband's temper. She had been seeing a counselor for three months for her depression and some vague physical complaints. Her husband Tom was seeing another counselor at the same counseling center, at her insistence. According to Tom, his wife was always in a "blue spell." She seldom spoke to him and continually fussed at her two children. She refused to go anywhere with him. Mary's counselor soon realized that she had hostilities of her own. She resented her husband controlling his family with his temper.

Neither Tom nor Mary could become angry without becoming hostile. He threatened and yelled. She burned with resentment. Since they had such a poor relationship, they could not tolerate the irritations and frustrations of marriage. They used anger and hostility to win recognition that was denied them in other ways. What each needed was respect and self-control. Both needed to stop their hostilities and begin doing something about their angers. Even though they expressed their angers differently, they had to gain control of their thoughts and behavior. The counselors helped them stop and examine their angers, what they were doing, and why. They helped them learn to think differently about their feelings and how they expressed them. With time and more counseling, Tom and Mary began to manage their angers. They learned what every angry person needs to learn, how to be slow to anger.

As we have seen, the usual responses to anger are to hold in the feelings or to let them all out in displays of temper. Even though there are problems with both styles of anger, they can be modified to be less harmful. Anger feelings can be held back and worked with, and not just buried inside. Dealing with anger feelings may mean developing a mental framework for accepting the stressful situation or deciding how best to express the anger to solve the problem. The solution to the problem of anger rests on both of these elements: taking control of anger by holding back (not in) and dealing with it by thinking and deciding about it. This is what the Bible means by being "slow to anger" (James 1:19).

Some psychologists refer to this reflective stage in the anger response as "inner dialogue."[1] One who holds anger back gains control of it and is in the best position to decide how and when to express that anger outwardly. Some people argue that anger is instantaneous and cannot be slowed down. One man told me, "When I am criticized, I immediately lash back out of control." But he should not let the speed of his anger responses fool him. Anger responses can be slowed down, if our counselees (and we who counsel) are willing to expend the effort. Emotional peace and satisfaction in relationships depend upon counselees making the effort to hold back their anger responses.

## JESUS' TEACHINGS ON ANGER

Jesus rarely got angry, even though people were continually attacking him or placing demands on him. He tolerated his disciples' stubbornness and stupidity. He understood their petty bickering about who was the greatest or their failures to understand his teachings.

He dealt with each person and situation individually and not from his own needs of the moment. He knew when to be forceful with Peter by correcting him for placing man's interests ahead of the cross, and when to be gentle, as for example, after Peter's denial. Jesus did not often become angry with the attacking Pharisees, but patiently answered their questions. He did not abandon his brothers, who doubted him, or Judas, who in the end failed to respond. He forgave his enemies at the moment they taunted him on the cross.

Jesus did show righteous indignation with the Pharisees when the temple and the message of his father was blasphemed, but gentleness, patience, and forgiveness characterized his life. He accepted his life and his lot from his father and focused on what was essential in life. He gave up his rights and privileges, and he kept people and events in a larger perspective. He "went the extra mile" and "turned the other cheek" with all individuals, and these two metaphors which came to characterize the founder of Christianity apply also to us who follow.

### The Sermon on the Mount

Jesus spoke clearly in the Sermon on the Mount about the need for people to rid themselves of anger. His use of specific expressions of anger (Matt. 5:21–24) and examples of situations that provoke anger (Matt. 5:38–42) suggest that he was not criticizing the one who felt angry, but the one who gave in to sinful expressions of anger. In this sermon Jesus turned his audience away from outward examples of righteousness to what resides in the inner person. Therefore, he taught that even though people may not have murdered or committed adultery, they still could not claim perfection before God, if inside they were angry or lustful.

75

Jesus said that everyone who is angry with his brother, or anyone who shouts "Raca" (an Aramaic term of contempt), or "you fool" is in trouble (Matt. 5:21–24). Jesus' forbidding the expression, "you fool," is not his presenting of a gospel of works more strict than that of the Pharisees. He was trying to convince the listener of the impossibility of perfect obedience to the law without God's power. It was this message of changing the human heart that would make obedience possible, even in people with seemingly uncontrollable angers.

In Matthew 5:30–42 Jesus delivered what can be called the "turn-the-other-cheek" teaching. He told his listeners to not resist an evil person, but to turn the other cheek (v. 39). If people sued them, they were to give them their coats (v. 40), and if they were commanded to bear a soldier's load the required mile, they were to go an extra mile. Jesus was not concerned with the injustice of bullies, law suits, or the Roman military, but with the attitude and response of the one wronged. The proper response in the face of mistreatment is not anger and hatred, but love and prayer (vv. 43–44). Jesus knew that the anger inside of people was potentially more harmful than anything the world could do.[2]

In teaching people to turn the other cheek, Jesus was saying that it is more important for people to have the freedom to ignore insults; then they are also free to decide how best to handle them. If people are angry and out of control, they are not free to forgive or to help others. They are also not free to walk away from danger.

The same desire for a peaceful heart is also seen in the example of the law suit (v. 40). Why should a man give up his last possession, his coat, when he has just lost a law suit and his other possessions? Jesus seems to be asking them to demonstrate that though they are angry, they are in control of themselves.

In Matthew 18:21–22 Jesus taught about forgiveness. Peter asked, "How many times am I to forgive my brother? Seven times?" When he said to forgive "seventy times seven," Jesus implied that people should forgive an unlimited number of times. And people are not only to love and forgive their brothers, but also their enemies (Matt. 5:43–48). This is the dynamic teaching of Christianity. Inner peace, forgiveness, patience, love—and all the benefits they bring to relationships—are the Christian goals.

God is often characterized as being a God of wrath, but this is only part of the picture of God and how he works in human history. He is also said to be slow to anger (Ps. 103:8; Neh. 9:17). This means that, though God has emotions, he is never out of control, but exhibits his righteous anger in accordance with his love and mercy. Being slow to anger is praised in man:

"It is better to be slow-tempered than famous" (Prov. 16:32 TLB).

"Don't be quick-tempered—that is being a fool" (Eccl. 7:9 TLB).

"It is best to listen much, speak little and not become angry, for anger doesn't make us good, as God demands that we must be (James 1:19, 20 TLB). Being slow to anger is praised because it is the path to preventing more anger (Prov. 15:1, 18).

The emotion of anger must often be held back, because its expression may be hurtful, and therefore, sin. And by holding back, a thoughtful approach that deals with the emotion and the cause may be taken. Some secular counseling approaches stress moral reasoning as an important part of the counseling of anger and violence. Raising a person's level of fairness, sense of justice, and concern for the needs and rights of others is helpful in stopping aggressive behavior.[3]

## SEVEN STEPS IN ANGER COUNSELING

What follow are seven steps that the counselor should take angry or bitter people through in order to help them become slow to anger. These seven steps are common to many anger-management counseling approaches whether the problem is temper, deep-seated bitterness, aggressive juvenile behaviors, or family violence.[4]

1. *Acknowledge anger.* The first step in this reflective control of anger feelings is for counselees to be willing to admit that they are angry. This requires acceptance of the naturalness of the anger emotion and one's own human limitations. The counselee has to know his limitations and that even these

weaknesses do not destroy his worth as a person. If our counselee lacks this sense of worth and does not know the forgiving nature of God, he cannot, in the rising heat of anger, admit that he might be losing control.

When people are wrong about something, they often become angry, because they are protecting their innocence behind the shouting.[5] The counselor can help angry people get in touch with their angers by getting them to talk about their hurts; this is helpful to those who experience violent anger episodes.[6] Counselees should be asked to share their hurts, and, therefore, see their angers and the reasons for them more clearly.

When working out the anger between two people or between clients and their counselors, it is important that angry people feel some freedom to express their negative emotions in the presence of others. We cannot learn how to express our anger properly, if we are always denying the fact that we are angry. This is a delicate thing to ask. Counselors must not confront people with the sin of their anger so harshly that they feel forced to deny what they are feeling. A counselor needs initially to create an atmosphere in which irrational and angry thoughts can be expressed.

The counselor might make use of group therapy for counselees with similar anger problems.[7] When people feel accepted and listened to, they are more open to the counselor's advice and more ready to learn about the negative results of griping. When they are able to slow down and realize that they are getting angry, then the door is opened for slowing down the growing anger feelings and stopping the anger process. While the initial feelings of anger arousal may not be sinful, raw emotional feelings may quickly become sinful thoughts. What begins as arousal or irritation may rapidly become feelings of bitterness or hate as thoughts give interpretation to feelings. It is helpful, therefore, to suggest to counselees some immediate action to slow down the rapid-fire thoughts that follow feelings of irritation. Counting to ten is the often-quoted advice. Relaxing is another. When persons feel the surge of anger feelings, they should immediately take deep breaths and try to relax their muscles.[8] They should think and talk slowly or not talk at all.

They should not necessarily take any immediate action, if none is demanded.

Sometimes, if possible, it helps to separate themselves from the conflict or the provoking situation. They should ask the other people involved for a postponement of the conversation and suggest a time and a place to continue the discussion. If no one else is involved, the angry person should try a change of scenery or activity. Someone who is getting mad because of a screw that will not turn ought to put the screwdriver down for a few minutes.

When a counselee senses that he or she is becoming increasingly angry, it can be helpful to recommend that the person try to play a musical instrument, listen to music for a while, jog, or watch TV. It may also be helpful to talk to a patient, listening friend or even to engage in calm self-talk.

These activities slow down the rising force of the anger and give the person time to think and plan what is best to do or feel or say. Alternative activities that raise the level of anger, such as pounding pillows, griping to another, or swearing to oneself should be avoided, since they do not create the mental environment for working constructively with the anger.

2. *Control thoughts.* Problems of anger begin as seed thoughts of self-pity, discouragement, jealousy, or some other negative thought. One's thought life is the *key ingredient in behavioral and emotional control;* therefore, thoughts prior to and during times of anger are important. Thoughts give emotional feelings prolonged existence and strength, and lend interpretation to vague emotions.

A stressful environment is not the first step to anger, but a person's thoughts prior to anger affect the degree to which stressful situations arouse anger.[9] A man who has good news to tell his wife may not be as aroused and irritated by five o'clock traffic. With a mind-set of confidence and security a wife will not necessarily have an adrenaline surge when her husband complains about the dinner menu. Changing the mind-set can be a practical therapy for aggression. For example, one research study showed that information about aging is helpful to those who abuse the elderly.[10]

When anger feelings begin, people should "listen" to themselves think. Their minds are constantly making value judgments, decisions, and comparisons. Therefore, there always exists the opportunity to intercept anger by changing these thoughts. Changing thoughts can be difficult, and our counselees will only succeed in this if they really want to control their anger. Anger-provoking situations arouse people emotionally, which tends to take the edge off of their rational thinking. Counselors should help people (1) to analyze what they are thinking and (2) admit it when they engage in irrational thinking, such as overemphasizing a threat or an offense. They also need practice at remaking their thoughts in the counseling office.[11]

Such rehearsal can involve restating an angry thought by leaving out derogatory adjectives or strong language. Another mental effort counselees need to make during times of anger is to avoid snap judgments. Feeling that others are the willful source of their problems will only incense them. Anger-prone people need to consciously realize that their "antagonists" are often trapped in their own responses too, and are not out to deliberately anger them. The following is an example of a thought pattern that needs such changes, which can be rehearsed in the counseling session: "That miserable excuse for a husband always purposely forgets and works late when we are going to my mother's! He acts as if he hates my guts!" These thoughts can be restated as, "My husband often forgets when it is time to visit my mother. I don't know if he does it on purpose, but it hurts my feelings."

Angry people must also remember that they are responsible only for themselves, and, in the long run, can only change themselves. The anger they feel rests within them and cannot be passed off by blaming others. The type of thoughts that characterize the slow-to-anger person are these: I accept the fact that I am angry, I accept myself in spite of my sinfulness, and I accept responsibility for changing myself, not other people. Even the painful memories of sexual abuse, which have given rise to anger and bitterness, have been healed by a person changing his or her thoughts.[12] Some counselors recommend that a person maintain positive thoughts as anger rises by directing attention elsewhere, such as by imagining happy, beautiful scenes.[13] While such neutral thinking may be marginally effective, it will have less benefit in helping to solve the anger problem itself. Correct thinking, however, in the presence of the problem we are facing, can produce lasting results.

3. *Discern the causes of anger.* Another step in the slow-to-anger process is to help counselees discern the causes of their anger feelings. Ask your counselees what is making them angry right now. Very often the provoking people or situations they describe are not the causes of their angers.

When a husband becomes angry with his wife after she tells him that the car will not start, he needs to realize that he is really not angry with his wife. In order to know how to control his feelings and solve the real problem causing the anger, he should look for the specific cause of his anger, such as financial worries. Being aware of the specific cause of anger does not involve a simple checklist, but requires some degree of self-analysis and honesty. The cause is not always other people or events; it may be personal fears, limitations, and irrational beliefs and expectations.[14] Such self-analysis cannot completely occur in the moments a person feels anger rising. Self-knowledge accumulates over time, making the task of discerning the counselee's role in his or her own anger easier. The person's needs and fears do not change overnight; therefore, some knowledge of the felt limitations and unmet needs can become important cues to what is really wrong.

Though a person's needs may be legitimate, the specific demands placed on reality or people for meeting those needs may not be. All of us need to feel secure; but to secretly demand that we never experience any car problems leaves us vulnerable to irritation and anger. Angry people need to recognize when they are making unreasonable demands of people or their environment, and, while not sacrificing their genuine needs, they should eliminate the demands that open them up to anger problems.

When we need to feel perfect or secure or in charge, our angers are directed at those people or events that seem to be interfering with the meeting of those needs. If we were sometimes forced to publicly admit what demands we were placing on others or on our environment to meet our needs, we would be embarrassed. We would have to say, "My time is more important than yours." Or "I want everything to work all the time," or "I do not want to hear about my faults."

Thinking about their needs and their demands can help angry people separate the fantasy demands they are making from genuine, just requirements for health, safety, self-respect, and communal living.

In discerning the causes of anger, people should not overlook their tendency to be involved in petty disagreements with those with whom they spend much time, such as their co-workers or their families. They should learn to ignore the small irritations and disagreements that come with being around people who are naturally different from themselves. There is a lot of peace-giving wisdom in Proverbs 19:11: "A man's wisdom gives him patience: it is to his glory to overlook an offense."

Angry people need to look to see if they have a chip on their shoulders, and learn to overlook an offense. Proverbs 17:14 says, "Starting a quarrel is like breaking a dam; so drop the matter before a dispute breaks out." A small irritation or careless word can lead to a serious argument unless it is dropped immediately.

Another common cause of anger is close association with anger-prone people. We can help our counselees by advising that they avoid habitually negative, complaining people, if at all possible. It is easy to become infected with another's dissatisfactions. Proverbs 22:24–25 appropriately warns:

> Do not make friends with a hot-tempered man, do not associate with one easily angered, or you may learn his ways and get yourself ensnared.

4. *Challenge irrational beliefs.* Being slow to anger means to mentally challenge any irrational beliefs or expectations and acknowledge correct ones. All of us have belief systems or mind-sets that assist us in making judgments and evaluating ideas, people, and situations. If we are frequently angered, we need to examine our belief structures.

For example, it is not helpful to expect children to always be good, or for cars to always run well, or for one's health to never fail. People should not believe that they are always right or that others are always selfishly motivated. They cannot expect their spouses and friends to always be cheerful or helpful or kind. Everyone should acknowledge that being ill and growing old are parts of life.

Also, people must realize that this is a fallen world and that this fallenness includes their own natures. The more people can align their expectations with reality, the more they can prevent anger from arising.

Irrational expectations or beliefs are not just mental errors, but are often a refusal to accept reality because we want things to be different for our convenience or purposes. Rational-behavior counseling methods focus on client beliefs and attitudes during treatment in order to help anger and hostility problems.[15] In such therapy, principles of rationality are outlined for the angry person. Old attitudes are evaluated according to these rational criteria and modified to new, nonhostile beliefs.

The Rational Emotive Therapy approach to anger stresses locating any irrational beliefs that people hold and showing them exactly how they can rid themselves of these beliefs.[16] According to Albert Ellis, the most common irrational ideas behind anger are the following.[17]

1. I must do well and win the approval of others for my performances, or else I will rate as a rotten person.
2. Others must treat me considerately and kindly and in precisely the way I want them to treat me.
3. The world (and the people in it) must arrange conditions under which I live, so that I get everything that I want when I want it.

Irrational beliefs that lead to anger often take the form of commands, such as: "This is awful," or "I can't stand this." Or, the irrational beliefs may be commands: "he should . . ." or "they must. . . ."

As their anger slows down, our counselees should challenge their irrational thoughts with statements such as:

• What evidence exists for this?
• Why can't I stand this noise or this unfairness?

- Is this person horrible, or is he or she just acting against my interests?
- Why should I get fair treatment at all times?
- Why must I always win or dominate?

If challenges to irrational beliefs are made repeatedly, whenever anger arises, then counselees will observe a change in their habitual ways of thinking about life and self and people. When beliefs fit reality, then anger becomes less of a problem.

5. *Do not be bothered by everything.* Being slow to anger means possessing a mind-set that allows people to recognize and accept the normal troubles that come with living and relating to others. People need to recognize that life can be unfair, that accidents will happen, that aging and death affect everyone. Angry people also need to be more accepting of people and recognize that they will have problems, bad days, and self-centered attitudes. Life is not perfect.

None of this is to say that people have to acquiesce to the threats of life, to lie down and not attempt to change anything. There is nothing wrong with positive thinking and the hope that today will go well or that people might repent and treat others better. But our counselees should not be shocked and angered when something does go wrong. Counselors should cultivate in angry people the attitude that life is something to work at and that problems are normal. Learning to laugh at normal failures and irritations has been shown to be effective in defusing anger.[18]

The book of Ecclesiastes presents a biblical world view that assumes that suffering, aging, and death are normal and accepted parts of life. The poetry of Ecclesiastes 3:1–8 creates an image of life under the control of a sovereign God. But this God-controlled existence still contains negative as well as positive events. The opponent parts in each poetic line tell people to expect both the good and the bad. "There is a time to be born and a time to die . . . a time to weep and a time to laugh, a time to mourn and a time to dance, . . . a time for war and a time for peace" (Eccl. 3:2, 4, 8). Ecclesiastes offers not a pessimistic view of life, but a realistic one.

In the second half of the book of Ecclesiastes (chapters 7–12) the focus becomes increasingly on the negative things, especially aging and death. This biblical view of life and its meaning argues strongly against expecting life to be perfect or other people to act only in pleasant ways.

Ecclesiastes warns that even a wise man can be corrupted (7:7), and that it is not smart to think the "good old days" were any better than today (7:10). Whenever people think that life was better and less irritating at an earlier time, they need to think about outhouses in the winter, no automobiles, no central air or heat. Life was undoubtedly filled with just as many troubles and irritations long ago. Ecclesiastes 7 relates this realistic picture of problems in the world to anger, when it says, "do not be quickly provoked in your spirit, for anger resides in the lap of fools" (Eccl. 7:9).

The same chapter also gives a specific incident that shows we should not let everything bother us. It reminds us:

Do not pay attention to every word people say, or you may hear your servant cursing you—for you know in your heart that many times you yourself have cursed others.
(Eccl. 7:21–22)

This passage tells us not to become angry if we overhear people criticizing us. We know from our experience of talking about others that folk usually do not mean what they say in those circumstances.

Anger-prone people need to concentrate on and appreciate people's good qualities. Even though people are not perfect, we might do well to change Will Rogers's famous saying, "I never met a man I didn't like," to "I never met a person who did not have some good qualities." People can avoid overreacting to the small hurts and disappointments in their relationships if they realize that disagreements are bound to happen in any normal relationships and that some disappointments and frustrations are bound to occur in the friction of relationships. Good relationships allow for such feelings, and we all need to practice forgiving and forgetting.

6. *Consider the goals for relationships.* When anger is provoked by another person, the counselee should be asked to think through his or her goals for the relationship in terms of the Christian's responsibility to love and serve others. This is true whether the relationship in question is with a spouse or an unknown passer-by or someone else. All of us have the responsibility to see that our actions reflect the character of God and that they improve our relationships.

Holding back anger also means having a forgiving mind-set.[19] It is almost impossible to maintain anger and a spirit of forgiveness toward someone at the same time. This does not mean merely granting people forgiveness when they apologize, but accepting people's limitations and faults. Granting forgiveness to others, whatever their sins or faults, is tantamount to recognizing that all human beings are frail and sinful. The forgiveness of Joseph, Stephen, and Jesus of their wicked enemies was a freeing grace which allowed them to decide how best to deal with their enemies. A forgiving person is able to consider the entirety of a situation, including God's perspective, and not just his or her own pain or hurt. Your counselees may have been treated badly and they may not be able to avoid hurt feelings, but that does not mean they are unable to control their anger feelings and replace them with better, more forgiving thoughts if they want to maintain the relationship.

In being slow to anger, people should also examine themselves and be willing to confess their responsibilities in anger-causing situations. Self-incrimination is difficult any time, but particularly in anger situations, when people may be facing accusations. No one in a relationship problem is ever totally innocent or totally guilty. With this belief, people can always keep the door open to their own faults without engaging in excessive, guilt-provoking self-incrimination. Holding back anger for even a short time and engaging in self-analysis in private has the effect of tempering the expression of anger. Confession alters our goals from changing others to changing the relationship, and to admitting that self-change and compromise may be in order. A spirit of humility and a sense of openness to being confronted help calm down the angry heart.

7. *Develop peace of mind.* Holding anger back and taking the time to work at changing anger responses develops an increasing sense of control and patience and peace. These attributes do not appear overnight, nor does anger disappear immediately. But it takes place over much time and through hard work, both in the counselor's office and in the middle of anger-producing situations.

Angry people need frequent encouragement by their counselors to be slow to anger. They need to develop and rehearse a correct view of themselves, of life, of other people, and of their goals for relationships. They need help from the counselor in accepting themselves in spite of repeated failures. And they need to be reminded to be responsible for their own angers. Angry people can then become people characterized by patience, which can be defined as a calm endurance and peace. Patience is a quality of remaining calm in spite of feelings of turmoil.

The weight of Scripture characterizes the mature person as one who is patient and calm and long-suffering. Meekness, humility, and love are to characterize people, not stubbornness, unkindness, or argumentativeness, which are outgrowths of unresolved anger.

Learning to be slow to anger moves us in the direction of Christian maturity, from which foundation we are more prepared for the loving confrontation required in all relationships and the righteous indignation required in a fallen world. Learning to be slow to anger gives us the time and freedom of mind to decide how we should solve our problems or how we should express our anger. Being slow to anger allows us to respond to conviction, to confess our sins of anger, and to rise above hate to forgive those who have offended us. From this foundation of holding anger back are made the decisions for how and when to express anger, for anger problems are not fully resolved simply because people hold back. Relationship problems in particular demand the proper expression of anger and the consequent resolution of problems. In the next chapter we will examine the proper way for people of patience, peace, and love to express their anger.

# CHAPTER SIX

# EXPRESSING ANGER PROPERLY

Men who bury their anger, and particularly Christian men who may think they should never get angry, find themselves suddenly shouting at their children and asserting their rights and lordship in the home. When their shouting produces only shouting or disrespect in return, many men resort to pushing or hitting their wives or children. One man who frequently abused his wife told me that he was not a violent person. But when he lost his temper and began shouting, he quickly lost control of himself. If his wife responded angrily to his anger, he just pushed her out of the way. Often, he could not stop and continued to hit her.

Women who lose control do not expect to push and slap their

husbands around; therefore, they push and slam doors, slap plates on the table, and stomp around the house. Such expressions of anger accomplish nothing and move those individuals further away from their goals of relating to people.

What is needed, during times of anger, is the knowledge of when and how to best express it. As we have seen in chapter 5, the knowledge of how to express anger must begin with what at first seems to be the opposite—being slow to anger. Being slow to anger is not the opposite of anger expression; it is the foundation for proper anger expression. Holding anger *back* is not holding anger *in.* Holding anger back is delaying the anger response to allow the mind to take charge of the anger response. That response may be silence or it may be loud, righteous indignation, but, in either case, anger becomes something that can be controlled for good purposes.

I suggested in chapter 5 that a spirit of peace, civility, politeness, and patience is more characteristic of the biblical view of maturity than expressions of anger. This means that overt anger expression may not often be desirable. But anger expression can be constructive, profitable, and without sin, particularly in relationships. Therefore, counselees need to learn how to express anger properly once the foundation of being slow to anger is present. "Anger-in" or suppressed anger has been implicated as a major culprit in hypertension and heart disease.[1] Learning to express anger properly has been shown to improve people's self-confidence, increase their willingness to discuss other problems, and give them a greater acceptance of other people's behavior.[2]

The first step that angry people have to take is to decide *how* or even *if* to express their feelings. Stopping to think about this and not just sliding automatically from the irritation to a public outburst, is being slow to anger. During this time, which may be brief or long, when people are controlling their thoughts, considering their goals, and reflecting on an accurate view of life and its purpose, they must consider what to do next.

A husband's outburst of anger at his wife is not the same reflex as yelling when a hammer smashes a thumb. A person must exercise control and decide if a response is going to occur. A wife may need to decide what to do when her husband leaves his dirty laundry all over the bedroom. Bitterness is not the answer; she may decide to let it go. Is it worth it to yell over this? There are more important matters, perhaps, to confront her husband with. Too many anger outbursts in response to small grievances are seen as nagging and serve no purpose. For her to unleash her anger at everything may be building the habit of anger without thought or control and it may also create unhelpful responses in her husband which interfere with more important confrontations later.

## ANGER AS RESOLUTION

Expressing anger feelings may occur as an attempt to solve a problem.[3] This is anger as resolution.

Our counselees need to see that their anger can aid in communication with and confrontation of other people. Anger as resolution, which does not have to be hostile or painful for another, can provide the motivation to change a bad situation; or it may help clarify to another how seriously one views an offensive situation. Anger as resolution involves an expression of hurt feelings in an attempt to keep a relationship strong and is not an attempt to hurt another or to get even. It does not involve any sinful expressions of anger, such as loss of control, name-calling, belittling or dominating another, or refusing to admit fault or to compromise. Anger as resolution is intended, not merely to relieve people of the pains of life, but to help them clean up the problems that bring those pains.

An elderly couple sought marriage counseling, after forty years of marriage, because the husband was filing for divorce. According to his wife, he had undergone a personality change. In the last four months he had treated her unkindly. He swore at her, ignored her, and, in general, did his own thing. Then, without warning, he filed for divorce. The counselor discovered that this man had forty years of buried resentment against his nagging, domineering wife, that now, for some reason, was coming out. He was angry and was expressing it. He decided, after forty years of marriage, to be his own boss.

The husband's feelings of anger were probably justified in this case, but what he should have learned in the many years of marriage was how to express the anger as resolution. He needed to know how to state his case, to identify his problems with his wife's style of relating, and to work toward a compromise. The counseling process itself can be a type of anger as resolution, where people who need training in this area can learn to identify their anger and how to express it constructively to another. Anger-management training programs have been used successfully for families, juvenile delinquents, criminal offenders, and mentally retarded individuals.[4]

### ANGER AS RIGHTEOUS INDIGNATION

Another form of anger expression is anger as righteous indignation, which can occur when significant injustice to people exists. The expression of outrage can contribute to solving the problem.

This is a difficult area in which to make decisions, but, in general, the injustice should be perceived against others and not the angry person, and involve serious moral, personal, or physical harm to people. Becoming outraged over receiving a parking ticket that was not deserved is not a case of righteous indignation.

The nature of righteous indignation may vary, but it should always be anger that is under control and is directed at a condition, not just at a person. Anger as righteous indignation should attempt to teach rather than destroy the offender. Righteous indignation is also unselfish, refuses vengeance, and is often reluctant.[5] In general, righteous anger should act out of love, not hate. If a person's anger is not of the type that would be labeled righteous indignation, then a counselee must recognize that his or her smoldering resentment or exploding rage is sinful, and it must be resolved as anger feelings.

An example of righteous indignation may be that which comes in response to child abuse or sexual abuse. Susan, whose husband was an alcoholic, was a mother of three children. Her husband had occasionally struck her when he had been drinking, but recently had become physically abusive of the children as his drinking problem worsened. One night, after he had knocked one of the children unconscious against a wall, this mother stood between her husband and her children with a large kitchen knife in her hand. She screamed at him and threatened him. Susan loved her husband. She felt sorry for him. She wanted him to get help and to be the man she once knew.

But Susan was frightened, and did not want to begin to hate her husband. She was willing to be beaten up or even to die for her children. Her display of anger happened two or three times and it always stopped her husband, eventually making him wake up and feel ashamed. He soon sought counseling help for his problem. Susan's reaction was righteous indignation.

Righteous anger is rare. It should spring from proper motives and it should be under control. Righteous anger should only come from people who are slow to anger, and who have learned how to handle anger by dealing with it inside or by expressing anger to resolve problems.

People need to be able to examine their motives, or the demands behind their anger, as they choose when and how to express their feelings. But the thinking process that involves the examination of motives cannot take place in the middle of a heated exchange. Counselors should help their counselees examine the demands of their anger.

Angry people should be asked if their anger outbursts are attempting to make other people feel guilty or to prove they are rotten? Are they using words that are intended to humiliate, dominate, or frighten people? Do they make threats? What purposes do the threats or ultimatums serve? Too many couples, in the heat of anger, suggest that they may not put up with the marriage for long. The threat of divorce serves no constructive purpose. It tends, instead, to reduce the relationship to a performance-based love and not the *agape* love of the Bible.

Better ways to express anger demands take the form of the following examples:

"My feelings have been hurt and I do not want to be hurt."

"I want you to understand where I am coming from."

"I think we can have a better relationship than this."

"Yes, I want you to change, but I am willing to change, too."

The emphasis in these demands is on solving the problem and not on attacking a person. The stress is on unmet needs, not on the specific, perhaps minor circumstance that may have precipitated the anger.

## THERE ARE GOOD REASONS FOR COMMUNICATING ANGER

One of the most difficult, but most liberating lessons to learn, is the wisdom required for expressing anger toward those who provoke us. Expressing anger *properly* does not mean that I must calmly and slowly explain my points of view. Anger expression involves anger feelings; therefore, proper anger expression might (and most always will) involve raised voices and vigorous debate. But it must always be in control, flow from right motives, and work for constructive change in a relationship.

The question is often raised as to whether an angry person ought to tell others when he or she is angry with them. While anger expression toward others is not always helpful, there are many good reasons for communicating anger feelings.

When a person is angry, that person has probably been hurt or frustrated in some way. Anger expression can give feedback to the one who provoked the anger so that person can realize how his or her behaviors are affecting others. A person needs this feedback in order to learn how to effectively relate to people. When someone expresses anger in words, even though the person is very agitated, a very clear communication is made to other people showing what is wrong. Communicating anger usually guarantees that the angry person will *not* feel the need to express anger in hostile, underhanded, or devious ways, such as through criticism, silence, or sarcasm.

It is not possible in close relationships with others to control and cancel all anger feelings. Much anger can be constructively held back, but to be "nice at any price" should not be the goal. A better goal is to work toward being a loving community, a loving family, a loving couple. Any relationship involves differences among people, different levels of maturity, natural misunderstandings, and the responsibility for assisting the growth of others; and in order to do the latter, people must mutually interact concerning their anger feelings.

When people express to others their hurt and disappointment in honest, controlled, and constructive ways, the other people are freed to be as honest with them. And growth in the relationship can occur. It is encouraging to us that relationships can survive and even improve when disagreements occur and are handled properly. Expressing anger properly also has the effect of exposing the angry person to criticism and challenge, and forces that one to stop blaming others and consider his or her own responsibilities for change. Neither suppressed anger nor explosive tempers provide the advantage that constructive expression of anger does when it opens one up to a critical evaluation of one's own behavior. Suppression and rage are, by comparison, cowardly ways of dealing with anger.

Proper anger expression should represent a turning toward fruitful negotiation, which becomes possible when people recognize that they are angry and when they try as clearly as possible to present the problem to the person perceived as responsible. This is the wisdom behind Jesus' teaching in Matthew 5:23–24 and 18:15–18, which says, in brief, that when another has something against you, you go and be reconciled; and when you have something against your brother, you go and be reconciled. Either way, mature people work out the anger between themselves and others.

There are also good reasons not to express anger to another. For example, it may be difficult to express anger to others without threatening them or heaping guilt feelings on them. Even skillful efforts at anger expression may only raise their defenses and further escalate the problem. Anger expression is also of little value unless the angry person is willing to go to deeper levels of a problem relationship. Anger expression must be seen as the *beginning* of honest changes on both sides.

Anger expression through physical exertion—such as jogging or dancing—may have some benefits when it is not possible to express it toward others.[6] The initial, physical response to anger is autonomic arousal with its accompanying tension and surge of energy. One strategy to restore homeostasis is to release excess energy through vigorous physical activity. Deliberate, harmless outbursts in private may also help people release tension. These could be stomping on the floor, hammering, striking a pillow, or screaming into a pillow. The biographer of Golda Meir said the prime minister took to polishing and rubbing her copper kettle in times of anger and frustration. But as we have seen, this aggressive expression may make people more aggressive, not less.[7] Apparently the beneficial effects depend on the conscious intent to reduce physical tension rather than on giving a physical accompaniment to fantasized hostilities.

When inanimate objects are the source of anger, not outwardly expressing that anger is the proper approach. No purpose is served by kicking a flat tire or throwing a golf club. There may not be any harm to kicking a flat tire, unless one breaks a toe, but being out of control in any anger expression is wrong. Throwing a golf club after a bad shot or swearing at a jar that will not open serves the building of a bad habit of uncontrolled anger expression.

## WHAT IS THE RIGHT WAY TO GET ANGRY?

Scripture recommends the cultivation of honest communication in relationships, and this implies that anger should not be allowed to build up inside. Proverbs 27:5–6 says that an "open rebuke" or "the wounds of a friend" may be very beneficial. And Ephesians 4:25 urges people to speak truthfully with their neighbors about their anger. Verses 25–27 in Ephesians 4 are instructive in a general way about the proper expression of anger feelings:

> Therefore each of you must put off falsehood and speak truthfully to his neighbor, for we are all members of one body. "In your anger do not sin": Do not let the sun go down while you are still angry, and do not give the devil a foothold.

In these verses we can see a threefold strategy to help a person with anger feelings. First, there are times when anger needs to be expressed. Second, it must be expressed without sin. And, third, it must be done quickly.

Saying that there are times to express anger implies that people must admit to anger. The time to express anger properly has not arrived until an individual acknowledges the anger and the responsibility for it. Expression of anger will not be proper if one blames the anger on others. Others may be the precipitating influences, but you and I are responsible for how we feel.

But how does one express anger without sin? Admitting anger and expressing it correctly helps people to avoid more subtle sins, such as criticism or self-pity. Expressed anger is open to others; thus it is more open to challenge and change. The expression of anger does not have to occur in the form of temper outbursts or other acts of hostility, such as verbal or physical abuse.

The third step is to settle things quickly. Whether we want to read this passage literally, "before the sun goes down," or just "quickly," the message is the same. People should not wait too long to deal with their anger, if it needs to be expressed. They should begin the process of being slow to anger and decide if and how that anger is to be expressed. To not express anger or to delay leaves one vulnerable to hard feelings. The greater the anger and the more important the relationship, the less time one can afford to waste not expressing this anger and healing the relationship.

## Honest Confrontation

Before those we counsel are prepared to express their anger and confront others, they may need help and training from the counselor in learning to speak assertively,[8] and in developing social-interaction and problem-solving skills.[9] I counseled a student who had a poor roommate relationship and constant angry feelings for that person. We spent several sessions rehearsing responses to the difficult roommate. She learned how to confront, to change the subject, to confess, and to ask for forgiveness. These rehearsals proved to be effective in improving her communication with her roommate. The counselor can use role playing and can rehearse counselees in behavioral as well as verbal responses.[10]

The following ten suggestions are intended to guide counselees in the process of confronting an individual who has hurt or continues to hurt or offend them:

1. Express anger to the other person in private.
2. Talk in terms of hurt feelings and not the other person's faults. In this way the other person is less likely to get angry or defensive and the angry person will get a hearing.
3. Keep the discussion to the central issue in question. Do not bring up all old grievances. If they exist, they may have to be dealt with at another time. Work on whatever situation precipitated the anger, and any causes for the anger.
4. Try to communicate and understand each other better and give up notions of winning arguments. Confrontation does not have to end in the other person's apology.
5. Share critical comments about the other person gently and in the same breath as positive qualities. This helps people listen to criticism without becoming defensive. We can take criticism better from those who respect us. Practice ahead of time how you will say things.
6. Do not exaggerate the issue or make threats about ending the relationship. Most problems are not that serious.
7. Allow the other person a chance to respond. Do not interrupt. Listen to what is said and look attentive. Do not just prepare your case while the offender speaks. Listening to the other side creates the climate for resolution and compromise.
8. When talking, paraphrase the other person's words. Make sure you understand the person and make sure that person has understood you.
9. If the other person becomes angry, try to be even more calm. Speak quietly and slowly. Give the person some time to get over the angry reaction.
10. Concentrate on moving toward a solution. Ask, how can the relationship work better in the future?

David Augsburger has aptly described the kind of relationships that can work through anger and become stronger by the proper expression of anger in confrontation.[11] Such relationships should be trusting/risking, loving/leveling, and caring/

confronting. They are trusting/risking because there is a balance between the ability to trust someone and the willingness to risk sharing anger. This means people can trust someone to hear expressions of anger without feeling rejected. Such trust allows them to risk expressing anger.

Good relationships are also loving/leveling, because love means being open before another. Leveling is the open sharing of a problem between two people. One of the most loving things we can do for others is to be honest with them. People need other people who love them enough to express their feelings without fear of destroying the relationship.

Good relationships should also be caring/confronting. A balance is needed between the responsibility to care for the needs of others and the responsibility to confront the issues between people. People who care will confront. When people care about each other and the relationship, the differences between them are important enough to become a part of mutual confrontation.

### Confession and Anger

Confession of anger, to God or to another person, may be the purest form of anger expression. Confession should involve an increased awareness of one's needs, motives, and faults. To admit that a particular situation or person is likely to make us angry is a helpful mind-set for preventing sins of anger expression. Confession is also needed in order to heal relationships and prevent further anger, when people have sinned in their anger expression.

Confession is an important part of confrontation and anger resolution also because people's anger has likely hurt or offended others. To apologize for bitter feelings or hostile actions and to take responsibility for what was done is a sign of personal strength and maturity. Honesty and vulnerability in confession helps those we confront assume a similar posture of humility and motivates them to repair the damaged relationship. Confrontation will be much better received if angry people are willing to admit their part in the problems.

Our counselees should learn to state, in simple and straightforward ways, that they were wrong. There is no need for them to apologize for anything other than their responsibility in the problem. If they feel they are not at fault in the problem they would be wise to consider admitting to the anger feelings they have toward the offenders, even if those persons are unaware of it. To begin confrontation over anger with an apology for that anger is an effective beginning. In such a confession angry people are admitting they are responsible for their own feelings. At the same time they open the door to discuss what provoked the anger.

Parents who have improperly expressed their anger to their children should apologize to them. An apology can be a wonderful opportunity for a child to see humility in action and to learn that parents love him or her even when angry.

A question naturally arises. Why should someone confess anything when the other person has been the offending party? Why should a wife, whose husband has had an affair, confess anything to him? He ought to be the repentant one. The answer is that the hurt party—the wife in this case—needs to do something so as not to be held a prisoner of hate and anger. Admitting one's responsibility for anger, even if it is only a confession to God, begins to free people from that anger. A woman may have a right to confront her adulterous husband with the anger, but she does not have a right to hang on to that anger. She may have been hurt so deeply that even with all the human strength she has, she cannot stop hating. But she should at least tell God that she wants to be free from her anger. The power to change comes when people admit that they have chosen to be angry and that they need to choose to forgive.

## FORGIVING THE WRONGDOER

Solving our anger problems and forgiving others are so closely intertwined that forgiving may be the most crucial step in neutralizing anger's destructive hold.[12] Anger as an emotional reaction is very difficult to change. People cannot just erase hatred or bitterness because they decide to; emotions are not direct products of wills. People can stop anger, however, when they *will* an equal and opposite response—in this case, to forgive the persons who offended them.

To forgive requires humility, which is the opposite of anger's self-centeredness. To forgive requires that we desire to improve a relationship and see another person benefit and grow. To forgive is therapy for the offended person, since anger is poison to the personality. It requires a sense of inner worth and security, as well as a strong will and the ability to empathize with the hated one. To forgive may be the hardest thing a person ever does, because the offended person is the one doing the forgiving.

Granting forgiveness is so important to emotional health and relationships that Jesus firmly commanded it in Matthew 6:12, 14:

> Forgive us our debts as we have forgiven our debtors. . . . For if you forgive men when they sin against you, your heavenly Father will also forgive you. But, if you do not forgive men their sins, your Father will not forgive your sins.

Forgiveness is also considered a powerful therapeutic intervention with the following positive results:[13]

- it frees people from their anger and from the guilt that is often the result of unconscious anger
- it helps people forget the painful experiences of their past lives and frees them from the subtle control of individuals and events of the past.
- it facilitates the reconciliation of relationships more than the expression of anger.
- it decreases the likelihood that anger will be misdirected in later loving relationships.

## The Steps of Forgiveness

One woman had plenty of reasons for anger at her husband. She had been married for almost twenty years when he suddenly abandoned her and their three children for a younger woman. The abandoned wife had to begin working to support her children, but her income was half of what her husband's had been. She was the sole parent to three teen-agers. Her husband, on the other hand, enjoyed his new freedom and drove an expensive new car. He saw his kids only when it was convenient for him. She was angry, more angry than she ever thought she could be, and it took her over seven years to rid herself of her hatred and bitterness. During those seven years she worked with a counselor who included the following steps in counseling her.

I give this example because I understand how difficult it can be to change any strong emotion. Even though I can list in this section the steps for learning to forgive and to resolve anger, this does not mean that anyone who reads this list will be anger-free in a short time. Anger and bitterness scars run deep, but nevertheless, people can defeat their anger if they learn to forgive.

1. Examine your heart and see your anger for what it is. Ask for God's forgiveness, if you harbor hatred and bitterness.
2. Admit to the reality of your hurt and other people's responsibility for it.
3. Pray that God will help you want to forgive those who hurt you.
4. Stop hurting the other party or engaging in acts of retaliation.
5. Try to forgive the offending persons in prayer. Do this each time thoughts of anger and bitterness surface.
6. Contact the other person(s) and seek forgiveness for any of your own wrongdoing in the conflict.
7. If the hurts are deep and the anger has been intense, meet with the offending party and openly express hurt and forgiveness.

Remember that extending forgiveness is of as much value, or more, to the offended person as to the offender. If the other people are not repentant, we need to forgive them anyway, at least in our minds, because we need to be free of anger's chains.

### How to Know You Have Forgiven

It may be difficult, at first, to know if a counselee has really forgiven another person. Emotions are not always dependent on willed actions. Angry people's feelings for their antagonists are not the best judge of whether they have truly forgiven them. To forgive is to enter a process of change in which the will of the forgiving person must be continually exercised. Professional counselor Ray Burwick suggests several ways to recognize if the people we counsel are not really forgiving the other party.[14]

1. Do they find themselves dwelling on the offense? Do the hurts often come back in their minds?
2. Do negative feelings and coolness still persist toward the person who wronged them?
3. Do they find themselves rationalizing the wrong behavior of the person who hurt them?
4. Does the bitterness spill over to others?

In general, people should expect their forgiveness of others to result in a lessening of the hurting memory. It is not always possible to forgive and forget, because the memory of the offense will still be there. But with forgiveness, the memory should become progressively less painful.

## Is Forgiveness Always Required?

Are there not some circumstances in which people cannot be expected to forgive wrongdoers, where the psychological scars of pain are too deep to ever be removed? For example, how can a woman who has been raped, or who has been sexually abused by her father, be expected to forgive such a heinous crime? Remembering the commands of Jesus and considering that forgiveness serves a purpose for mental health (to free people from bitterness and anger), people must try to forgive even when they have been hurt deeply. Since forgiveness is an act of unselfishness, and unselfishness is the opposite of sin nature, we must expect that such forgiveness becomes possible only as a person matures in the Christian life.

Such forgiveness may be the greatest act of love that a bitter person could offer one's greatest enemies, and therefore, the most difficult thing he or she could ever do. Without God's help I would agree that such forgiveness is not possible. But with his help, one's nature can be transformed from self-centered to

God-centered, and loving the enemy can be a reality. There is one thing worse than a serious crime such as I've mentioned, and that is to let the crime and the resulting hatred continue to plague and destroy a person.

Learning to forgive takes time and effort, but it can be done. In the Old Testament, Jacob's son Joseph had reason to hate his brothers (Genesis 37–50) for they sold him into slavery. He missed his father very much. He ended up in jail and grew up in a foreign land. But when we see Joseph in the Old Testament account, he is not a person of hatred or resentment. He is free to make the best of his situation and is, therefore, open to God's use. When he meets his brothers later in life, he overflows with tears of joy and compassion. That is the freedom that every person who hates must strive for.

Victims of physical abuse sometimes feel guilty and unworthy even though they were not responsible for the abuse. In some cases of sexual abuse, for example, men and women use hatred and anger to combat their own guilt feelings for the way they have been hurt. A young woman's guilt feelings may interfere with her ability to forgive her sexually abusing father; but instead of using hatred to protect herself, she should correct her unworthy feelings. She was not responsible for the sexual abuse!

In cases like these the counselor needs to give counselees time to work through anger and move toward forgiveness. The anger and hatred are certainly wrong, but counselors and friends must continue to stand alongside enraged people and see them through to the freedom of forgiveness.

## The Results of Forgiveness

With genuine forgiveness, resentment and hatred are replaced by joy and love, and the barriers between people are removed. Forgiveness does not erase the memories of past offenses, but strips them of importance. The factual part of the memory remains, but the painful emotion is gone. Forgiveness sets people free from past memories and present fears, frustrations, and anxieties. Forgiving others allows our minds to focus on the present and its concerns with all of our emotional energy. Forgiveness gives us the satisfying joy of relationships, from the normal conversation of a parent with her son's teacher to the deep relationships of marriage and family. Forgiveness also gives us a more compassionate look at the sins of those around us. If we really forgive the past, then the present is considered in the same light. Forgiving someone means understanding someone. People of anger and resentment are always running into more things to make them angry. It may be tough to forgive, but the alternative is worse. Anger and resentment can only harm. Forgiveness brings life.

# CHAPTER SEVEN

# COUNSELING AND ANGER
# IN MARRIAGE

Gene and Paula have been married for nine years and have two children. They came to see their pastor for counseling for two reasons. Gene complained that their sex life was dead. Paula said she was suffering frequently from depression. After several sessions with Gene and Paula, their pastor began to see a variety of causes for anger in their marriage—causes that were common in married couples with whom he counseled. However, Gene and Paula could not resolve their angry feelings; they vacillated between buried resentment and explosive outbursts and were unable to communicate their feelings to each other in any other way.

Paula was irritated by the children and frequently lost her

temper. She felt overworked and unappreciated in the home, and resented the fact that her husband did not help around the house. Gene, on the other hand, felt that he was as good a husband and father as anyone. He thought he rarely "lost his cool," but resented his wife's constant complaining and nagging. He found it easier to ignore her than to listen to her problems, and he never confronted her with his resentments.

Paula grew less friendly with Gene and sex became infrequent for them. When he did initiate sex, they did not get far, because she would start an argument. Attempts at sex now became opportunities for both Paula and Gene to unload years of buried resentment on each other. As bad as their arguments were, this fighting was their only form of serious communication. The arguments made them realize that they had problems, and that their resentments and bitter arguments were not going to disappear without help.

## MARRIAGE: THE MAD FACTORY

Perhaps in no relationship is the understanding of anger and the principles behind its cure needed more than in marriage. Marriage is the most intimate and perhaps the most complicated of human relationships; in marriage, irritations, hurt feelings, misunderstandings, impoliteness, and overt selfishness often occur. Disagreements are normal and even inevitable in relationships, and so we are not surprised at their appearance in the marriage relationship.

Each family is unique. Think of the variety of sex, age, size, temperament, need, ability, and interest—in just one family! Unlike a business corporation or a church, the family is not tied together by one central purpose uniting disparate individuals. Its members eat, sleep, dress, and relate to the outside world all in close proximity to each other. The husband and wife must make a broad range of decisions, from spending money, to handling emergencies, shaping goals, deciding on a menu, or selecting a television program. To expect perfect agreement all the time between husband and wife or parents and children is unreasonable. Such perfect families and perfect marriages exist only on television.

Marriage forces us to meet other people's needs and to submit our own vulnerabilities to others. Being locked into a marriage forces one's self-centered nature out into the open, where disagreements and arguments take place. Growth and maturity follow the working through of problems and disagreements. Staying away from people or not relating to a spouse may mean less anger, but it will also mean less maturity and love. So many marriages fail, not because people have married the wrong people, but because they are not *being* the right people. Marriages thrive out of self-surrender and compromise.

More than in any other relationship, people need, in marriage, to learn to be slow to anger. They must hold their anger back and decide, with common goals in mind, how best to work through disagreements. They need to learn how to express their hurts in marriage without fear of rejection and without hurting their spouses. Marriage needs an atmosphere where anger and hurt can be expressed without fear of counterattack. The marriage partners must learn how to properly confront one another when one is hurting the other. They must learn how to confess their limitations in the marriage, and how to forgive, for anything and everything. Unfortunately, for many people marriage is a battleground; for some it is the scene of abuse.[1]

The first thing that Gene and Paula's pastor did, after giving them opportunity to express their anger and frustrations to each other in his office, was to remind them of what a Christian marriage is all about. When questioned about their marriage, both Gene and Paula said they felt that the other person managed his or her respective responsibilities very well. Paula thought that Gene worked hard and was a good father; Gene felt that Paula was a good mother and homemaker. But neither one had bothered to communicate any appreciation to the other for a long time.

Marriage is more than a good working relationship. God intended marriage to meet some of our deepest needs, including the need for love and security. To meet those needs, a person has to draw close to the other partner through a process of self-surrender. The romantic feelings we have at the beginning of marriage make self-surrender easier to practice.

But, when those romantic feelings change over time, as they must, and as the work of marriage increases with children, illness, or financial problems, the married person must work hard at self-surrender for the sake of the bonding of two into one flesh.

The pastor asked Gene and Paula to remember the strong romantic feelings for each other they once had. He made them write down the qualities that they still appreciated in one another. Gene and Paula had forgotten that they were wedded together in *holy matrimony*, in a relationship that could be a person's closest contact with another human being—not merely a work relationship.

## THE CAUSES OF MARITAL ANGER

Consider the multiple causes and situations where anger can be born and fester in a marriage. Married people grow accustomed to their spouses and tend to take them for granted. They know the relationship can be one of intense love; therefore, they place high expectations on their mates and suffer disappointments when those expectations are not met.

Marriage can be physically exhausting, especially when children are involved. A mother's anger is affected by the age and presence of children in the home, by how much the husband helps, and by the amount of contact she has with friends.[2] The physical demands of home and family on women are great and are understood by few men. Women live in an environment of stress, loneliness, and simmering anger.[3] Many also suffer fatigue and other symptoms from too little sleep, premenstrual syndrome, and improper diet, and those who balance a job outside the home with family responsibilities report high levels of hostility.[4] Young couples also may face, in marriage, severe financial pressures and when those limitations press in, disagreements are almost inevitable. Many husbands become irritable when faced with bills to pay, because the money never seems to go far enough.

Newly married couples have many reasons to bury their anger. They have high expectations for themselves and want to be the very best people they can be in marriage. If they are Christians, they have additional expectations concerning

Christian maturity, which normally include selfless love and avoiding the sin of anger. Before marriage, they have probably seen each other in a limited number of circumstances. But after marriage, every irritation or disappointment of life is on display before another person.

Burying their anger cannot go on for long. Before the end of the honeymoon or certainly before too many months have passed, serious temper outbursts can occur. Unless the two have had good experience in handling their disagreements in dating, the presence of so much temper and resentment in marriage is shocking and disappointing to them.

Married couples need to see two levels of the causes and cures of anger. The first is a surface level and relates to personality characteristics and learned styles of communication. Couples obviously need to talk to each other and work through anger feelings in an atmosphere of open, honest, and constructive communication. Very few of us learn the skills of communication needed for marriage in our previous family and friend relationships.[5] Nothing quite prepares us for marriage except marriage. Therefore, in the early years of marriage a couple needs to work through irritations and learn how to communicate with each other. Arguments and resentments are not the end of the world, nor do they mean that people do not love each other. They are opportunities to spot and correct problems, and to get on with the business of loving each other.

But there is another level of the anger problem that needs to be addressed, and in fact, it is the heart of the anger problem. We all are fallen human beings with self-centered natures. We see reality from our own perspectives and therefore, selfishness is the result. All the teaching and workshops on communication styles, verbal strategies, listening, "power talk," and nondefensive self-defense will only be of marginal help if self-centeredness continues to reign. Seeing the human anger problem as merely a failure to understand or to communicate leaves people with organizing a "cookbook" list of steps or "how tos" on dealing with anger.

Many books, including this one, will have lists of things for counselors and their counselees to work through. The problem is that surges of anger are sudden and take only seconds to reach emotional peaks. At those times, people do not have the time nor the inclination to pull out a list of ten steps for dealing with anger. Solutions to anger in marriage have to be seen, not just as principles to follow, but as changes of character to be developed. This chapter and this book are not about stopping anger, but about helping people become more patient and loving. People often lose their motivations to change in marriage, because it requires persistence, and the fear of divorce may be the only factor that makes a couple work on anger problems. What people need in marriage is a change of heart, the ability to be loving and patient and peaceful.

## BEING SLOW TO ANGER IN MARRIAGE

Since negative feelings toward a spouse coexist alongside loving feelings, a husband or wife needs a strategy to deal with the negative feelings before they crowd out the loving ones.

The question naturally arises: Should I opt for total openness and share all my hurt feelings with my spouse, or keep negative feelings inside in the interest of getting along?

The two options are not good choices. In the first instance, persons may only be dumping their feelings on the spouse. Or, they may be refusing to work through their anger when they keep it within. Neither of these is acceptable in marriage. What is needed is a method of working with anger feelings that neither violates the nature of marriage or its goals, nor attacks the self-sacrificing love relationship of the couple.

In chapters 5 and 6 I have already outlined the biblical strategy for dealing with the stream of angers that flow from normal marriages. Spouses need first to hold anger back and reflectively work with it. In the mind the temper can be calmed, resentments can be eliminated, future anger prevented, and words of confession and forgiveness crafted. As people hold back and become slow to anger, they are more prepared to engage in the necessary expression and communication of their feelings, tensions, and problems in the marriage.[6]

### Be Prepared

Archie Bunker of "All in the Family" frequently told his wife Edith to "stifle" or "dummy up," when he did not want to hear what she had to say. Edith did stifle and dummy up, until she could not hold it in any longer. To talk about holding anger back in marriage does not mean to stifle or dummy up. It means people should take control of their anger and reflect on its causes and possible expressions before deciding what to do about the feelings.

Holding anger back means that married people think ahead of time and prepare to avoid anger-causing situations, and that they make up their minds not to let certain circumstances bother them. Holding back means being prepared, knowing what to expect in their mates, forgiving ahead of time the faults they will show. Holding back is purposing to do all that one can to remove irritations from one's spouse's life. It is purposing to not use certain forms of anger expression. There is never a reason for married people to strike or threaten each other. Counselors must help couples look carefully at the typical forms of anger outburst and counsel them to avoid all shouting, stomping, name-calling, and door-slamming.

## Change the Scene

Holding back anger may mean that when a person sees anger coming, that steps be taken to avoid the stress or provocation. Husbands and wives can learn to abandon an argument before it begins, by changing the subject or walking away.[7] Later, when they are more calm, may be a better time to discuss the issue. They should not just walk away when their spouses are talking to them; but they can admit it when they are getting angry and would like to continue the conversation later.

A mother should occasionally walk out of the room away from her misbehaving children. With a few minutes of silence, she can calm down enough to decide how and what to do. A husband would be well-advised to frequently get his wife out of the house and away from the kids, so there is time to talk, to listen, to show concern, and in general, enjoy being alone with his wife. This can fortify the wife to manage unruly children.

## Admit to Being Angry

In order to hold back and reflectively deal with rising anger feelings, husbands and wives must admit that they are angry.

They should not feel embarrassed or ashamed about that, for those are natural responses. Anger feelings in marriage are warning signals that people are being hurt and are in danger of not responding well.

The easiest way for people to develop a habit of admitting their anger to themselves is to learn to immediately express their honest feelings to God in an attitude of humility and with a desire to deal correctly with their anger. This does not mean necessarily expressing pious words such as, "I am very angry. Please forgive me." To honestly admit anger may require something that more exactly fits what is felt. "Lord, I'm so mad at my husband! I know I should be sorry, but I can't help myself. He has hurt me so much! I do not know what to do. Please help me!" The person who admits anger is prepared to begin to take control of that anger.

**Drop It**

Psychologist Larry Crabb, in his book *The Marriage Builder*, advises couples in dealing with anger feelings to consider subordinating the public expression of their feelings to the goal of allowing God to use them for his purposes.[8] Crabb feels that the emotional *acknowledgment* of anger is always proper, but the emotional *expression* of anger is only appropriate when it does not conflict with fulfilling God's purposes in our lives.

We must decide in every situation in which we are angry with our spouses whether expressing our anger to anyone but God will serve God's purposes. Relationships like marriage can give people the freedom to vent their anger without the fear of losing love; but a marriage will not thrive in an atmosphere of anger. The marriage relationship may tolerate wrath and bitterness, but its wounds from the same are deep. Married people can disagree without being rude and hostile. Just as alcohol can be an excuse to lose one's temper, so too, marriage, and being behind closed doors, too often becomes an excuse for "letting one's spouse have it."

Couples who are mature in their handling of anger and conflict know when to keep quiet about trivial matters and when to argue for the sake of things important to the relationship. It is often sound advice to do nothing about being irritated or angry at one's spouse. There are too many irritations and conflicts of interest in marriage to get angry at every one of them. What people should not do is to wear their spouses out with the continued expression of trivial angers so that important matters are ignored when they arise. On the benefits of holding anger back, Carol Tavris writes,

> In the final analysis, managing anger depends on taking responsibility for one's emotions and one's actions: on refusing the temptation, for instance, to remain stuck in blame or fury or silent resentment. Once anger becomes a force to berate the nearest scapegoat instead of to change a bad situation, it only loses its credibility and its power. It feeds only on itself. And it sure as sunrise makes for a grumpy life.[9]

It would be hard to say more clearly that holding anger back can be very positive; but perhaps the words of Scripture say it best: "a gentle answer turns away wrath . . ." (Prov. 15:1).

## The Married "Mind-set"

Married couples may be slow to express their anger, but their thinking should be anything but slow. They should actively think about what they are feeling and why and what are the options they have in dealing with its causes. The thoughts and beliefs that control responses to anger in marriage are what I call *the married mind-set*. It is this mind-set that will help people interpret each situation and the feelings they are experiencing. This mind-set will also help people interpret or read into other people's actions.

If my view—my mind-set—is that anger cannot be controlled, or that my spouse must change her personality—if I say to myself *I'll only take so much of this and then I'm out of this marriage*—then I have negatively affected my ability to control and express my anger. A proper mind-set, on the other hand, can positively affect my views of the world, including marriage.

The most important attitude to develop in my marriage, in order to control anger, concerns my desire to change my spouse into what I want. Counselors regularly encounter the man or woman whose desire or insistence is that the marriage partner be a certain type of person. You will hear your counselee say, "he needs to be the spiritual leader in the home, " or "she ought to meet my sexual needs," or "he should spend more time with the kids," or "she never takes an interest in my work." These are not illicit desires for change. In fact, we could find biblical support for change in all of these directions. But a mind-set that requires that one's happiness, and the health of one's marriage, depends upon changes in the other person is a faulty one.

There are other propositions that people hold that are obviously false and only destine them to more anger feelings. Some of these propositions are: "I have a right to do what I want," or "my purpose in life is my pleasure and happiness," or "conflicts should be avoided at all cost," or, "I don't make mistakes; my spouse should know what I need," or "I'll only do as much work as she does."

Time may be well spent if we can help marriage partners bring their beliefs that lead to anger into the open and guide them toward acquiring new beliefs. A healthy mind-set for guarding our counselees' temperaments during the irritations and angers of marriage include the following:

1. People change people by loving them and by giving up the strategy of changing them.
2. Disagreements and conflicts offer great opportunity for achieving understanding and intimacy.
3. Leading from "weakness" (honest admission of doubts, fears, and problems) strengthens a relationship.
4. Commitment to a marriage does not depend upon every need being met or on a partner's attitudes or behaviors.[10]

These are some of the most important foundational beliefs in marriage: the conviction that Christ will meet a person's needs, and the knowledge that one can and should love his or her spouse regardless of the problems. This is what self-sacrificing love is all about.

Our counselees should be aware of their responsibilities in

making the marriage work. Each must also have compassion for the marriage partner, forgiving and sympathizing with the person's weaknesses. The twin abilities of accepting other people's limitations, and being aware of one's own, contribute mightily to the peaceful married life.

A counselor can help married people list their spouses' faults and then accept them as they are, without change. I may hope that my spouse will change, but I will not require it before my love is given. Our counselee should look upon his or her marriage as a chance to serve another person and make that person happy. This mind-set makes people slow to anger, giving them the patience to choose how they should best express their anger. Perhaps no better mind-set to curb anger toward spouses exists than the one expressed in the wedding vows: "I take thee to be my lawfully wedded husband (wife), to have and to hold from this day forth, for better, for worse, for richer, for poorer, in sickness and in health, to love and to cherish, till death do us part."

Crabb suggests that the marriage partners will do well to distinguish between the desires each has and the goals they mutually hold for their marriage.[11] For example, each desires the love and respect of the other. When this rightful desire is fulfilled, each feels secure and significant to some degree. But lacking that, one feels hurt.

Goals, on the other hand, are different. Crabb notes that some folk make it their goal in marriage to change the other person. But this cannot be an acceptable goal. Rather, the man ought to make it his aim, or goal, to minister to his wife's needs whether his own needs are met or not—and vice versa. They can't assume responsibility for changing one another; if one sees something that needs changing in the other person, he or she should ask God in prayer for that. Goals are the things people can attain by their own efforts, such as learning not to mention some petty matter. But desires—such as wanting some change in the other's behavior—cannot be realized by one's own efforts. In marriage, a person must do those things that minister to the other spouse and avoid working for those desires which merely seek to change the person.

When we are irritated or angered by something our spouses

have done, we have to ask ourselves whether expressing our anger to the other person fulfills a goal or a desire. We need to ask what our anger is all about. According to Crabb, if we can express our anger in an attempt to accomplish the goal of a strong and intimate marriage, then we should do so, but if it is merely an attempt to get our partner to change and meet our needs, then it is not appropriate.

This does not mean that we can never express our anger when our spouses have mistreated us. We can confront our spouses if we can see that the confrontation can help to minister to them. It is proper for us to express our angers to our spouses for the purpose of preventing bitterness between us, or for making ourselves more understandable, or giving feedback concerning our actions. But our goal in sharing anger can never be to hurt or to change our spouses.

While Crabb's approach on sharing anger with a spouse may seem restricting, let us remember that it is an ideal. In the meantime we are not powerless to talk about our needs and desires in marriage. We should express our angers and desires to our spouses, but always with the pledge that if these desires are never met, we are still committed to love and minister to them as our partners. It is, therefore, to our counselees' advantage to work to express anger properly, pursuing the mutual goals of the marriage and making personal desires secondary. Subjugating personal desires is not easy in marriage, but it is necessary in order for married people to meet each other's needs.

## EXPRESSING NEGATIVE FEELINGS WITH ONE'S SPOUSE

To be avoided in expressing anger is the uncontrolled emotional outburst in which the other person is attacked. This is the most difficult anger expression to avoid, and the most frequently violated principle in resolving conflicts. People simply let themselves get out of control, but nothing has been solved. These outbursts can be turned into constructive expressions of anger feelings if some basic principles are followed.

As counselors we should help married couples practice these principles during the counseling sessions:

1. Have couples express their anger feelings while both man and wife are sitting down, looking at each other. They should maintain eye contact. In this way one is seen as talking to another person—a beloved spouse—and not to an object of one's frustration.

2. Encourage each counselee to talk briefly. Then each should wait for a response, and act in an interested manner. Angry people should not act as if their partners are on trial and they are the prosecuting attorneys.

3. Let them focus, not on the other's character, but on the objectionable behaviors. They should talk more about their own hurt feelings and less about their partners' problems.

4. Tell them not to argue in public. If people cannot wait to vent their feelings, then they are not prepared to express anger properly.

5. Point out that angry people should stick to the main topic(s) and avoid inflammatory language that moves the dialogue from constructive sharing to emotional dumping.

6. Tell each to keep calm if the other spouse chooses to unload on him or her. Tell them to listen and not be defensive, reminding them that everyone calms down eventually. A married couple needs to look for compromise and a solution to the problem, each acknowledging one's own faults, admitting them aloud and being willing to apologize.

7. Help counselees concentrate on their feelings of forgiveness for their spouses, even while they are thinking of how they have been hurt. Even in the middle of an argument, angry people must mentally compete with their feelings of hostility and keep anger under control. They should not think of their spouses as *the* problem, but as *having problems*.

8. Recommend to the couple that they use a conference time for the regular discussion of tensions and grievances that surface in the marriage. This can begin during counseling sessions under the counselor's supervision. Suggest that the husband and wife go out to eat once a week with the purpose of asking how things are going, and of airing

any grievances that need to be raised. Tell them: Keep it light, friendly, and businesslike, anything but tense and hostile. If an argument begins at home, the couple should retreat to the kitchen table, imagining themselves at the counselor's table, and proceed to listen to one another. A regular time for discussing issues and tensions can help eliminate the habit of arguing just to get a hearing.

9. Advise couples to pray together every day. Counselors can help them begin this practice at the beginning or end of each counseling session. Things shared in prayer before God and a spouse have a way of being softened and put into a larger, spiritual perspective. It is hard to concentrate on self-centered impulses when kneeling before the Lord and praying for a mate. It is easier to remember at that time that a spouse is God's gift, to be loved and to help develop in the likeness of God's spiritual image.

Now that I have listed these principles, let me remind us of this: solving problems of anger is not a matter of memorizing and following principles, but of helping people change into the persons these principles represent. Such a change does not occur overnight. It is hard work, too. Right in the middle of an argument, or immediately after, we do not want to love. We may not feel we cared if our mate dropped off the face of the earth. But deep inside, we do care, and we need to find ourselves again—our peaceful, kind, patient, loving selves. Marriage is not making my spouse the right person, but it is both of us becoming the right persons.

# CHAPTER EIGHT

## COUNSELING AND ANGER IN CHILDREN

Christie is an angry twelve-year-old. Her parents were divorced when she was seven and her mother remarried several years later. A youth pastor discovered that Christie is mad at many people in her life because of the divorce and because of her feelings of rejection by her father and her fears for her future security. She is angry with her father for cheating on her mom and abandoning her. And though she likes her stepmother very much, she is angry with her also, because she was the "other woman." Christie is angry with her stepdad because he is not her father and he takes her mother's time away from her. She is angry with her mom, because she somehow let the divorce happen, and with a younger sister whom her dad seems to favor. And that is not all; now she is mad at her boyfriend who shows an interest in other girls. Christie is angry at nearly every important person in her life and her joy is being squeezed away.

Christie's counselor led her to examine each of her relationships in the light of her parents' divorce, so as to better understand her anger and more responsibly assign its causes and constructively express it. In Christie's case, she had to come to grips with her anger at her father and work it out, and stop developing anger for everyone else involved.

## A CHILD'S ANGER

A child's anger is not like adult anger in one very important way. Children have flashes of anger, but they do not usually carry grudges. In other words, they easily forgive.[1] Part of the reason for this virtue lies in the child's limited perspective on life and small storehouse of memories. Each day is fresh and new to the child. Life is relaxed. Children take life as it comes and then let it go.

In one observation it was found that, among toddlers, conflict involved overt aggression less than 25 percent of the time. In six- and seven-year-olds, physical attack happened only 5 percent of the time; and verbal attack took place 40 percent of the time. The majority of conflicts among preschoolers were settled without adult intervention, and play resumed 75 percent of the time with little or no upset.[2]

Children are more humble than adults, because they can accomplish so little on their own. Humility makes forgiveness possible. In addition to forgiving as quickly as possible, children also respond to pain with the appropriate release of crying rather than anger.[3] Children also like to give things to people or to physically reassure them or hug them, if a relationship is strained. Our children are always drawing pictures with I-love-you messages for my wife and me, if we have been angry with them. As a rule, children do not like it and are emotionally harmed by parents who hold on to grudges and anger for hours or days.[4] Not forgiving is the opposite of relating and loving. Unfortunately, it is not long before children begin to model the ways of adults, and long-term resentment begins to affix itself to

120

their personalities. Verbal and indirect methods of retaliation tend to increase with age in a child.[5]

Children and teen-agers, just like adults, need to express their negative feelings. Considering though that children have much less training and experience in understanding and handling their emotions than adults, and considering their many frustrations, difficulties, and the lack of control over their lives, they do quite well with their angers. Children do not have to be taught to get angry, but how they may express anger is progressively shaped by their parents, family, and peers.[6] If young children are punished or meet with vocal disapproval every time they express anger, they may grow up habitually suppressing anger.

The most important role of parents in dealing with anger in children is teaching them how to control and express it. Anger in children is not something that simply goes away if parents use the right discipline techniques. Frustration, disappointment, and physical and emotional trauma are a part of a child's life and do not disappear with maturity. Dealing with anger, however, is not a part of the child's natural responses to life. Therefore, counselors can help parents teach their children how to deal with anger by the methods they use in discipline and by dealing properly with their own angers.

We should not expect the child of a good, loving home to be free of anger. Frustrations in meeting needs and dealing with physical limitations raise every child's anger level. And children are more likely to lose their tempers around the family than anywhere else. Family members who are loving and sensitive are a known quantity; it is safer to lose one's temper at home than among strangers. Family members are also the ones who give or withhold the things or the love each child needs.

Therefore, children may be polite to strangers but terrors at home. Very early, children show the ability to control their tempers depending upon where they find themselves. My wife and I are always amazed when school teachers or baby-sitters tell us how well-behaved our children are. Around strangers they are nearly perfect. But around mom and dad they occasionally feel free to let us or a sibling "have it" when they are angry. We feel encouraged rather than discouraged by their temperamental behavior, because it indicates that they are learning to control themselves. Home is a place where every family member feels more freedom to "sound off." That openness is not entirely bad, as long as parents are not encouraging emotional self-indulgence.

In dealing with a child's anger it is important to remember that anger feelings are not necessarily wrong. When a baby cries or a two-year-old shouts a definite "No!" they are not necessarily being bad kids. The expression of anger in thoughts, words, or deeds determines the sinfulness of the anger emotion.

Young children are less prepared to evaluate the appropriateness or sinfulness of their anger responses than adults. They depend upon their parents' training in order to begin to analyze and correct their behavior. Angry children are not necessarily bad children, but are in a process of learning, and this learning will continue through the teen years. To expect children to learn to banish every anger emotion or to get along perfectly with their siblings and playmates is to expect something that parents themselves cannot manage. I stress innocence in a child's anger, because it is very important for parents to see angry children with compassionate eyes. A child's anger may be a problem or it may just be an irritation to parents, and therefore, our problem.

## PARENTS AS MODELS OF ANGER

The natural reactions of adults around children seem opposite of what they ought to be. Children's anger irritates us parents, who tend to shut it down quickly and angrily. Parents hope that the child's anger will just go away because they forbid it, and often it does disappear behind slammed doors and under buried resentments. What children need are compassionate teachers. Their "classroom" is crowded with daily lessons of parents' angers or their own.

Anger between adults in the home puts great stress on young children and tends to increase their own aggressiveness.[7] In experiments, children have been exposed to live models who expressed anger toward each other. The children who witnessed this anger experienced heightened arousal and showed an increase in verbal aggressiveness in play. Some subjects experienced sadness upon observing adult conflict and wanted to intervene. Others experienced anger at the angry couple.[8] The younger the children, the more likely they are to attribute adult conflict to something they (the children) have done.[9] Angry, punitive mothers tend to have children who are angry and noncompliant and who distance themselves from their mothers.[10] Children of angry parents also tended to be less empathic when witnessing the distress of others.[11] Mothers who have irritable infants tended to respond with irritability and anger of their own, increasing the infants' crankiness, making a vicious circle of anger followed by anger.

Counselors for anger problems in children need to work carefully with parents to solve the problems by beginning with parental aggressiveness.

Children need patient, understanding parents who model communication, honesty, self-control, confession, and forgiveness. They need mature parents who do not overreact to them or against them. Teen-agers are in special need of parents who understand the growth toward independence and the self-identity search that come packaged with so many angers. Parents must learn how to manage their own angers and then to operate from that position of strength to teach and model before their children.

## CAUSES OF CHILDREN'S ANGER

Children become angry for basically the same reasons as adults: Anger is a response to the frustration of not having the world the way they want it. Children face a variety of external demands and pressures. They are dependent on others and physically unable to defend themselves. They are emotionally inexperienced and are not equipped to handle rejection, nagging, confusion, embarrassment, boredom, schedule changes, older siblings, or dead pets.

Kids learn to use temper and grouchiness as a technique for manipulating others. Shouting and crying brings them attention which reinforces temper outbursts. Their anger is related to whether they feel liked or not.[12] Hormone levels in boys,[13] affect their anger as well as whether or not they think their misfortunes are because of others' hostility toward them.[14]

## Sibling Rivalry

Sibling rivalry is a major source of anger in a child. This is in part due to the frustrations that can enter the child's life when another child or two is competing for the same space, toys, or parental attention. The only child may have a more peaceful life, but the child with older and younger siblings is learning the socializing skills of assertiveness and compromise.[15] Anger can be the motivation for a child to learn to relate to others. Unfortunately, children can also employ anger to manipulate each other.

One of the greatest needs of parents is the wisdom to know how much to let children manage their own arguments. Parents must teach children how to give in and how to compromise, but also how to assert their rights. Older children need to know how to defend themselves against younger siblings without "killing" them. Parents cannot tell older children to leave the younger sibling alone and then allow the older ones to be pestered. Younger children need to be assertive without taking unfair advantage of being small. The youngest ones need to know that they are not alone and that they do not have to fight all their own battles.

In spite of all the crying and the "don't touch me! Mom, he's on my side of the room! She's licking me!" and the name-calling and practical jokes, siblings can be good friends and generally love each other very much. Parents should help them stay that way.

The Bible story of Joseph and his brothers makes parents aware of another problem causing sibling anger, and that is jealousy over parental attention. Nothing is more painful to a child than to feel less loved or appreciated than a brother or sister. Joseph's cruel brothers were not model siblings when they sold Joseph into slavery, but their father Jacob had been insensitive in showing obvious favoritism toward Joseph.

We can only speculate, but Cain's problems with Abel could have been related to Cain's feeling less loved by God, and by Adam and Eve. Author John Steinbeck used this idea in *East of Eden*, in which several characters relived the emotional pains of Cain and Abel. The best thing parents can do for sibling rivalry is to relate to each child individually and, therefore, differently. Each child is a unique person with individual gifts and problems. We do not need to compare children and thus challenge their self-respect. Parental love should be given equally to all children, but it may be individually given.

## Perfectionism

A related source of anger in some children is the burden of perfectionism. Children who discover that their acceptance depends upon their performance may strive to be perfect for their parents. They seek, by their relentless pursuit of perfectionism, to keep their parents and other adults happy and loving, and they fear any failure as a threat to their security. When these children fail to reach their goals, they become angry or depressed. Such children need to learn to admit and live with their limitations, to realize that they do not have to win praises and love from adults.

## Children's Anger as Communication

Anger in children, as in their parents, must be seen in part as an attempt at communication. All anger contains information to which people need to pay close attention. Anger in children is especially important because they are still developing their skills in communication.

When a young child says, "I hate you, Mommy," he or she may really be saying, "I am very angry." Parents need to remind themselves that their children's angers may be forms of *need* statements. Their children's angers can be manipulative maneuvers, attempts at control, or prolonged programs of attrition, putting mom or dad on the defensive for some real or imagined oversight or injustice. Divorced parents often deal with this.

Anger may be the only way for children to express their feelings initially. People need to listen to those expressions since they can tell the observer much about the children's needs. Could angry children be frightened, or sad? We need to pay attention to a child's tone of voice and facial expression and physical movements or stance.

Both parents and counselors of angry children must try to get children to express their feelings by supplying appropriate words or suggested actions for them. Many children get angry when they are embarrassed or when they feel threatened by new surroundings. Parents should talk to their children about what they are feeling and why. Some children simply need more sleep, and adults have to be able to see that in their anger and grumpiness. Whatever the reasons, a child's anger demands vigilance and work on the part of parents—and who else will be more committed and more loving to see children through their anger problems?

## Anger at Parents

In many homes, parents are the main source of frustration and anger in their children. Because of their own frustrations and anger, parents can fail to communicate trust, affirmation, and love to their kids. What should be normal, enjoyable relationships between parents and children become, instead, a constant series of confrontations. Children are hurt and angered by their angry parents and express their anger in ways designed to hurt and frustrate in return. If this continues into the teen years, the home situation becomes intolerable to both parents and teens.

Children's hostility to parents has been increasing in recent years because of the increase of physical and sexual abuse in the home.[16] Divorce also results in anger at both parents, as we have seen in the case of Christie. It is interesting that children of divorce who are cared for in joint custody rather than only the mother's custody show lower hostility toward both parents.[17] This may suggest that mothers, particularly, bear the brunt of the unending pressures from small children and adolescents, often with little or no reward. Teen mothers, especially, react to this pressure with silent endurance, broken occasionally by outbursts of temper and hostility, often all out of proportion to the child's "crime."[18] The periods of silent endurance are characterized by the parent's angry thoughts toward the children, and then shame and depression for having such thoughts and for failing to be a better parent. It is no wonder that counseling anger in children often involves counseling angry parents also.

Children are not fooled by the sullen, unfriendly, begrudging attitude of parents and they respond to it with whining and disruptive behaviors.[19] Older children, in their anger at mom or dad, even know what to do or not do to "load the gun" for mom or dad's next outburst of temper. This anger breeds more, and the parent-child relationship is strained.

Parents need to learn that they cannot push children into perfect patterns of behavior. Child abuse and neglect are correlated with the myths of what children should be like and what parents find unacceptable about themselves.[20] Kids are kids. They will never be perfectly quiet or polite. Bedrooms do get messy, flower pots get knocked over, burping contests do get started at mealtimes. Two-year-olds say no to everything, nine-year-olds talk back occasionally, and thirteen-year-olds think they are twenty. This is not to say that parents cannot teach, guide, discipline, scold, or spank their children. But it does mean that they should expect childishness to precede maturity, and emotional outbursts to precede control.

Parents should be careful to not permit the anger to become a stumbling block to their children. This is why the Bible warns, "Fathers, do not exasperate your children: instead, bring them up in the training and instruction of the Lord" (Eph. 6:4) and, "Fathers, do not embitter your children, or they will become discouraged" (Col. 3:21).

## THE GOAL OF INDEPENDENCE IN CHILDREN

Children have a strong, natural drive toward independence which parents must learn to honor and accept as well as manage. This strong drive, though, often works against the mutual dependency and giving relationships in the family. Children will strive for their autonomy, and it is not possible nor desirable for parents to try to stop this. What parents can do is to assist their children in the gradual development of independence and decision making. This will fend off much of the anger that develops when children lock pubescent horns with their parents. Morality, a goal parents have for their children, is based upon the child's ability to choose independently of other people's knowledge or desires. Children must sooner or later reach maturity and claim their faith and behavior as their own and not just in order to fulfill their parents' demands.

While autonomy is a necessary goal of growing up, too much autonomy may lead to frustrations. This is because total autonomy is tantamount to loneliness, whereas a certain amount of dependence keeps people in relationships that give emotional warmth and security. Every child needs a parent's help in finding the balance between autonomy and dependence at each particular age, in order to avoid negative emotions and confrontations with adults. Young children should be allowed and encouraged to do things for themselves and to take responsibility for their own actions. At times this may look like a power struggle with parents, but when wisely managed and tolerated, this struggle becomes the fodder of personal growth.

## ANGER IN YOUNG CHILDREN

Infants must enter the world complaining. They get uncomfortable, hungry, hot, and wet. They have gas, colic, fevers, and bad dreams. Some complain a little, and some a lot, but crying and fussing are two of the few forms of communication available to the young child. To the infant who is uncomfortable, anger and rage may be the only ways to convey that fact. Parents need to understand that rage in an infant generally means the baby is hungry, wet, tired, in pain, or uncomfortable. The baby is not being bad. It is just being a baby. Language will not be a possibility until the infant reaches the second birthday, normally.

Since a habit of anger is easy to develop in a baby's life, it is important that parents work to meet an infant's needs or remove discomfort and associate good feelings with mom and dad's presence. This does not mean that a baby should be fed every two hours at night in its first year, simply because it cries. An infant needs to develop regular habits of sleeping and eating, and some frustration of needs will be useful for this. Often, nothing seems to calm a crying baby, and parents have to pay careful attention to their own angers at these times. It is advisable to walk away from a screaming infant and regain control of anger feelings, or to hold and walk with the baby and thus learn to tolerate crying. These responses are preferable to allowing frustration to build because nothing one does seems to help.

When a child grows older, the anger problem is usually not one of crying rage, but of temper outbursts. A two-year-old often defies parents with a resounding "No!"

When one of our sons reached the age of two, we thought that he was sick, because he was so hostile to people. But when we realized why "the terrible twos" were so named, we learned to accept them as a normal part of child development. Often, when children give a defiant no, they are not rebelling at all, but are having fun being different and watching how parents scramble to react. Saying no makes two-year-olds feel powerful for the first time.

I remember when my wife and I took one of our sons on his first bus ride at age two. He enjoyed the fifteen-minute ride enormously, but when we got off the bus he was enraged because the ride had ended. He stomped away from us down the sidewalk. Being a psychologist with my first child, I told my wife to let him go. He would soon look around, feel insecure, and come running back to us. Wrong! I underestimated the strength of childhood anger. After walking one block he was still going strong and we had to race after him in order to stop him from crossing a street. He must have felt his power, because I certainly did not feel mine.

Counselors can help parents learn to handle anger in children. When young children rebel in anger, parents should ignore their no's and talk about the issue they are insisting upon. Mom should forget a child's display of anger and talk about the need for bedtime, or a nap, or whatever the issue is. A parent can give the child a choice: "Would you like to read a story and then go to bed, or go to bed without a story?"

Parents should not try to argue with a child. To battle a child's anger and defiance—no for no, anger for anger—will only lead to more frustration, anger, and defiance in the child. Sometimes the no of a child is only an expression of a hidden fear. For example, a child who refuses to go to bed may be afraid of the dark. Parents should always strive to know and understand their children well and then, not out of anger but out of wisdom, decide when to assert parental authority.

## The Temper Tantrum

Counselors are often called upon to give advice to parents whose children throw temper tantrums. There is no mistaking these children. They scream or hold their breath, and throw themselves on the floor, kicking and pounding. They may even throw things or attack people, though that is rare, because such responses are more likely to lead to parental retaliation. This fact suggests what many parents of tantrum throwers suspect— the tantrum is a calculated display of anger to control parents.

Tantrums generally appear in a child between the ages of three and four and fade away within a year. They are the result of a child's high level of energy and low self-control. The child's loss of emotional control is deliberate, since most tantrums occur only in a particular place such as home or school but not both, or with a particular person such as mom but not dad.[21] This violent display of rage usually ceases in children as soon as they get their way. The fate of the temper tantrum depends on the patience and behavior of the target parent.

Parents need to possess enough discipline themselves to not give in, but to stop the temper tantrum and all future ones. We can encourage the expression of a child's anger, but not tolerate the child's acting aggressively. The ventilationist theory of anger works no better for children than for adults. Letting little Hilda blow off steam does not make her a peaceful little girl, but only encourages more steam-blowing later. We should forbid screaming, kicking, hitting, and biting, but encourage the child in expressions of feelings and disappointments that seek to relate to us adults instead of dominating us.

Counselors should instruct parents not to allow themselves to be held hostage in public by a tantrum-throwing child. Parents should make up their minds that they are going to forget embarrassment and act swiftly. First, they should not allow children to hurt themselves or someone else. If they are in a store, and calm, firm talking or holding does not work, then they should remove the child, going to the car or a restroom and swiftly administering discipline. Parents should make it clear to children that they will not get what they want by such behavior.

An angry child can often be diverted from anger by changing what is occurring at the time. Suggest to parents that they change the child's activity. If he or she is frustrated in trying to color well, send the child outside, not to kick trees, but to do something else. Many children are poor sports or have a hard time losing at board games or athletic contests. In such cases, the best therapy is for parents to be good models. Parents should show their children how to lose gracefully and be happy at the good fortune of others. Parents who lose their tempers are not helping their children's anger problems. Parents should let their children win at Candy Land or Chinese Checkers, but should also play to win themselves sometimes. Children need both experiences. Emphasize fun and character and skill building, rather than winning or losing.

Whatever the temper situation is in a child, when the storm has subsided, parents should spend time with the child to discuss what caused the anger and how it can be handled better next time.

### ANGER IN ADOLESCENTS

To be emotional and easily angered at parents is a common characteristic of teenagers. Adolescents are experiencing social and physical changes that are difficult for them to adjust to. Insecure within themselves, they often react in anger to their parents as a way of gaining some sense of control over life. Teens vacillate between being children, who need warmth, security, and advice, and adults, who are secure, confident, and in control. Once-docile and obedient children must turn into teens with minds of their own. Counselors should stress with parents of teens that the struggles their children face in the teen years are inevitable. The growth toward autonomy cannot be arrested, but how parents and children deal with the challenge can be changed.

Fortunately, parents of teens have had years to learn patience and to establish good relationships with their children. When a teen becomes disrespectful or sassy or extremely argumentative, the parent should be in a position of character in which anger is not required. Heated argument does not work with the teen-ager. Parents may rule with anger and authority, but they are only postponing the problem. Parents must realize that teens are changing the way they think and are learning to make new decisions almost every day. They are also changing emotionally and are not always best at rational thinking and decision making.

This is the time when teens need parents the most, and parents need to keep an open door for communicating and relating. Counselors should help parents of rebellious teens learn to keep calm and be flexible, to set limits, say no in love, and be forgiving. Parents should know that teens will lose their tempers occasionally, but that is not the end of the world. We parents should not let these years be ones in which we hurt our children and deny them love and understanding. Angry teens need patient parents as models and teachers and guides into adulthood.

### TEMPER TANTRUMS IN ADULTS

Many adults, just like young children, make effective use of explosions of anger to attempt to get their way. The tantrum may also take the form of constant pouting or the silent treatment. Such people make a habit of handling their anger in the same way every time. Temper outbursts serve as their communication to others and make them feel better. The problem, though, is that everyone around them is hurt by their childish anger.

Counselors should deal with a temper tantrum in adults in much the same way as with children, except, of course, that the adults cannot be restrained or disciplined. Screaming adults are not completely out of control. They can hear. They can reason. We should ignore their bizarre behavior and talk softly and slowly with them. Accept the fact that they can be angry, but do not be manipulated by the outburst. Push the adult with temper tantrums toward talk; let him or her discuss the feelings of hurt.

In general, counselors should overcome angry people with goodness (Romans 12:21, Matthew 5:39), keeping in mind what is ultimately good for them. Show acceptance of angry people without necessarily agreeing with their right to throw a tantrum. Speak reasonably, slowly, and rationally in contrast to their more exaggerated forms of communication. Pray that you will not become defensive, that you will hear them out, and that you will know what to say. Once the tantrum throwers have calmed down, get them to talk and think about what they are feeling and what should be done about it.

## GUIDELINES FOR COUNSELING PARENTS WITH ANGRY CHILDREN

The following guidelines are suggested with the hope they will prove helpful for counselors to share with parents who struggle with angry children.[22]

1. Parents should see that young children get plenty of rest, especially during strenuous family outings or vacations.
2. Parents should give children their attention when the children are hungry, bored, tired, or feeling left out or oppressed by others.
3. Parents should let children know what parents consider inappropriate displays of anger and what consequences they can expect.
4. Parents should not make children apologize while they are still angry. A forced apology is not an apology and only serves to make the child resentful and angry within. Wait until a child has calmed down and sees what was wrong with his or her behavior.
5. Counselors should encourage parents, more than anything else, to love their children. Love will cover a multitude of the sins of both parents and children.[23]
6. Parents can help children understand that their anger feelings are not bad. They should not tell their children not to get mad; it is unreasonable to expect them to never get angry. To feel anger is quite normal for any age.
7. Parents can help children admit to and vocalize their anger and then point them toward working on solutions to their anger and not spending time just venting feelings.
8. Parents can help children decide on constructive versus destructive patterns of expressing anger in the home.

9. Parents should teach their children a philosophy of life that helps them deal with the frustrations of life, including relationships and character growth. Christian parents have to communicate to their children that Christianity is more than church on Sunday. It is a way of life that addresses their problems in living and relating.

# CHAPTER NINE

## COUNSELING AND ANGER AT SELF

The people in life we most frequently get angry with are probably ourselves. We become angry when we embarrass ourselves in public, or when we fail to do something we know we have the ability to do. Anger at ourselves occurs when we repeatedly serve double faults in tennis, or when we lock our keys in the car or oversleep and are late for work. We get angry at ourselves when we eat four pieces of chocolate fudge instead of sticking to our diets.

In all these examples, we are disappointed in ourselves; we expect more from ourselves than what we are doing. This anger at self may be expressed just as anger at others is expressed.

Most of us have gotten mad and called ourselves names, or looked at ourselves in the mirror and frowned.

Anger at self is usually suppressed without any exterior manifestation. It can be wrapped up in feelings of guilt or depression. It has been shown, for example, that among college students compulsive eating is significantly related to indirect hostility, irritability, and resentment.[1] When we receive second letters from a relative and have not responded to the first letter, we feel a surge of disappointment in our performance. We feel guilty when unfinished work piles up. It bothers us that we do not share our faith, or tithe, or have daily devotions.

Some folk may harbor shameful sins or habits and continue to wallow in them. In general, people feel that they are not the perfect persons they ought to be. This quiet disappointment in self is anger which feeds a low self-concept and which has the same disturbing effects on personality and relationships as does one's anger at others.

At its worst, anger at self relates to such psychological problems as depression, extreme loneliness, and suicide attempts.[2] These problems are most likely to occur when disappointments build up and other people treat us in ways that reinforce our low self-images.

Lori came to see me because she lost her job; every area of her life seemed to be falling apart. As we met regularly over the next several months, it became apparent that she was suffering from such a low self-concept that she was aiming her resentment at herself in an attempt to punish herself.

Lori's problems seemed to stem from her religious parents who stressed that, as a mature Christian, she should no longer have any sins. Of course, the Bible does not teach that, but during her teen years, whenever she failed in some way, she doubted her salvation and went forward in church to the altar once again. She would also increase her efforts in the outer works of religion, such as Bible study, prayer, and witnessing. At times she spent hours every day in prayer and went witnessing several times a week; no one in her church could equal her fervor. She attempted to pay for her "sins" by making herself look ugly. She purposely acted stupid, so that she would not have any friends or dates.

What Lori needed was a sense of worth and freedom to be herself. What she received instead was a constant message that she was untalented, ugly, and sinful. Therefore, she began to punish herself so that she might earn God's favor. She made herself fail at everything and this made her hate herself all the more. Years later, she had lost several jobs because she suffered from obsessive thoughts that interfered with her ability to work. Those obsessive thoughts related to her self-hatred and her eventual rejection of religion; while she blamed religion for her guilt feelings, turning her back on her religious upbringing caused her more guilt.

## HOW A POOR SELF-IMAGE RELATES TO ANGER

Anger at self is part of a vicious cycle that includes a poor self-image. Persons with a poor self-image on the "inside" have to strive harder on the "outside" to make up for it. Outer behaviors and accomplishments become very important to such people and any failure becomes a disastrous message to self. If we have adequate self-images we can tolerate occasional defeats and can honestly reflect upon self-limitations because our self-concepts are secured elsewhere. But those with poor self-images are more likely to ignore the truth about themselves and pass the blame on to others. Such people are prone to get angry with others and blame them for their own shortcomings. Simple hurts or faults or frustrations become major anger situations to persons of low self-esteem.

A person with a poor self-image uses anger to protect self. In an extreme example we see this happening in cases of rape or incest. A victim's feelings of worthlessness or self-blame are so strong that she will use an intense anger against God or the sexual offender in order not to be overwhelmed by a sense of worthlessness and shame. Low self-esteem also correlates with problems of spouse abuse and child abuse.[3] Therapies for violent men help them discover options and opportunities for feeling good about themselves so they feel in charge of their lives without having to dominate and humiliate others.[4]

In general, people with a low self-concept tend to grow more angry at others and at frustrating environments. They are acutely aware of anything that interferes with their goals, and they also have higher standards for people around them.

The other side of this self-image-anger coin is that people who are habitually angry have a lowered self-concept because they see visible signs of their failure and spiritual immaturity. They set higher standards for themselves and others, which lead to more anger episodes and more problems with self-image. They have become trapped in the anger-self-image cycle.

Two biblical examples of people who were angry at themselves are Haman, in the book of Esther, and the apostle Peter. One of them strove for greatness, but his anger was his undoing. The other was helped out of his problem with self and went on to greatness.

Haman plays the archvillain in Esther's story. He alone is angered by the Jew Mordecai's refusals to bow down to him. He is incensed and insulted by what apparently does not bother the king or his closest advisors. Haman, who is constantly trying to put forth his own glory, sees Mordecai's actions as a threat to himself. He is so angered that he plots to destroy millions of Jews in the empire and is even willing to pay a fortune to do it. Haman's ruthless pursuit of glory and power raises the possibility that he was operating from a poor self-image. In the end, Haman hanged on his own gallows.

Peter, the apostle, suffered from self-rejection, but found the secret of peace and self-acceptance. After his denial of Christ and the subsequent crucifixion of Jesus, Peter wept bitterly at his own failure. But his disappointment in himself did not lead him to deny his failure or to attempt great acts to compensate for it. Nor did he belittle others to make himself feel good. In the aftermath of the resurrection Peter accepted the unconditional love of Christ and the commission to serve Jesus as he was, failures and all. When unconditional love and acceptance from others and from oneself become the basis for inner security, then inner peace replaces hostility. By contrast, a poor self-image leads to anger at self and others. This may be why the ten apostles became indignant at the two who wanted the highest positions in Christ's kingdom (Mark 10:37–44).

Anger tries to protect a weak self. A loved and accepted self, on the other hand, is free to admit to limitations and faults and seek the path of peace.

## THE BIBLE'S TEACHING ON SELF-IMAGE

The relationship between anger and self-image is a two-way street. A low self-image can lead to anger, and being angry and out of control can lower one's self-image. If people have poor self-images, they tend to be angrier at life's frustrations, setbacks, and insults, because these seem to challenge their worth even further. This is why a mother with rejection in her childhood is more likely to be a hostile parent.[5] When people get angry and explode, they have an even lower view of themselves, a view that says they are failures, immature, and out of control. To solve the problem of temper and resentment, people need helpful, accurate counsel on self-image and how to keep it strong.[6]

The biblical teaching on self-image is not to be found in any exhaustive concordance under the subject of self-concept or self-love. Self-image teaching in the Bible resides in the unlikely word *humility*. Humility is the biblical word that carries the meaning of our self-concept. But humility deserves a careful definition lest people too easily come away from the Scriptures with an inaccurate view of self.

In its teachings on humility, the Bible does not say, "Low is me, walk on me, nonassertive all the way." On the contrary, a humble view of self can be defined as an accurate view of self. In Philippians 2:3–9 people are encouraged to follow Christ's example. He knew he was the God of the universe and yet he did not consider that fact something to cling to. When people know themselves accurately and accept themselves with strengths and weaknesses, there is no need to prove who they are at others' expense. In fact, with a humble, accurate view of themselves people are free to love their neighbors as they love themselves.

Thus, people are commanded, "Do nothing out of selfish ambition or vain conceit, but in humility consider others better than yourselves. Each of you should look not only to your own interests, but also to the interests of others." This passage does not say that others are better than self, but that the humble person, with an accurate view of self, is free to treat other people as if they are better. People are not told to forget their own interests; humble people who know their strengths are free to consider someone else's needs. Humility leads to love, not anger.

The humble view of self is an accurate, God-centered view. A person who has a talent such as singing may know in all humility that he or she has one of the best voices in the church. That is not pride. It is the truth and the person need not prove it to anyone.

This humble view also recognizes that one could be wrong, or that someone with a better voice could join the church. The humble person does not have to hide ability nor deny it. Humility keeps people from feeling the flames of anger when the choir director picks someone else for the solo part. A humble person does not have anything to prove and, therefore, does not have to get angry. With a realistic view of self one does not stumble into the anger that pride causes.

Another aspect of the biblical teaching on self-image is the teaching that God accepts individuals the way they are. People are loved and accepted by God in spite of their faults. This uncritical acceptance by God is rooted in the mystery of Christ's death on the cross, which people need not fully understand to believe or to experience in their lives. We need to accept ourselves for what we are, God's image on earth, under development toward an eternal glory and fellowship with God and with each other. People should eliminate standards of comparison such as beauty, intelligence, or money, which are destined to be lost anyway.

A person also needs to accept oneself in spite of the sins in his or her life. I can move away from failure and be accepting of myself without necessarily being satisfied with sin in my life. I need to exercise compassion in exactly the same way when I see the sins of others. The willingness to accept oneself should make it possible to view with the same eyes of compassion a neighbor's struggle. Therefore, self-acceptance leads to an understanding of others' faults and less anger toward them. The whole process is a cycle in which people move from accepting themselves to accepting their neighbors; and when neighbors respond and treat them with more patient accept-ance they grow even further in their self-acceptance.

## SELF-ACCEPTANCE AND ANGER

To counsel with a hostile or bitter person often requires counseling that person's poor self-image. Persons with a good sense of who they are, and what their strengths and weaknesses are, do not have to use anger to feel powerful. For those low in self-image, the feelings of power provide a temporary elevation of their own importance and a lowering of someone else's status. This is why one of the best methods of producing anger in experimental subjects is to put them in a situation threaten-ing their self-esteem.[7] But the experiment is short-lived and has to be repeated over and over for them to continue to have feelings of power.

Anger gives the angry person a false feeling of self-confidence, but only while the heat is turned up. When angry people "sim-mer down," they begin to have doubts about themselves. They feel guilty for their part in the problem and sense some degree of failure in their own personalities to deal with conflict and to control their emotions.

Angry people, especially those with problems of self-worth, are not helped if their anger statements are immediately re-jected or ignored without a hearing. Such treatment makes them feel even more small and discouraged than before, and their anger is likely to grow. When people share their angry feelings with us as counselors, the best thing we can do is to respect their rights to their feelings. If our response tells them—"you have no right to be angry"—then we are not help-ing them deal with the problem.

This does not mean that when angry people complain to us as counselors that we have to agree with the complaints. The coun-selor should give the angry complaint a hearing and then make suggestions about how the counselee should respond to the problem. A listening counselor contributes to the person's sense of self-worth, thereby helping the person be more prepared to listen to suggestions. The responsibility for anger sharing is not entirely in the hands of the counselor or friend on the receiving end of the anger complaint, however. If people want a hearing from others regarding their anger, they have to help by turning down the anger volume and by giving their counselor or friend a chance to listen without being threatened and without losing respect for them.

## PRACTICAL STEPS FOR DEALING WITH ANGER AT SELF

Counselors can help those who are angry at themselves by working through the following anger-management steps with them.

### Recognize Anger at Self for What It Is

Anger at self is nearly the same as anger at another person. Counselees will find it easier to work with negative feelings when they can identify them as "anger," rather than attempting to find a handle on a nebulous "self-image problem." They can challenge the anger in their thoughts and behaviors, but feelings of low self-worth seem untouchable.

Counselors should teach clients to distinguish between being dissatisfied with themselves, or wishing to improve in some area, and self-anger. Self-anger spends more time loathing self than thinking of constructive ways to change. Self-anger gives up and wallows in depression, hopelessness, and negative thinking. The key to dealing with anger at self is to recognize that one can find fault with oneself without robbing self of worth, because self-worth does not come from being beautiful, perfect, or sinless. Self-worth comes from being created in God's image and from his declaration of human value.

### Set Realistic Expectations for Yourself

When we begin to feel inadequate in some area, we often devise severe measures to help ourselves shape up. The motivation behind this is good, but the expectations we adopt for ourselves are often so unrealistic that we set ourselves up for more failure. There is nothing wrong with setting very high standards; but they are not helpful if we cannot tolerate a less than perfect performance. The pastor who goes to work each day with a to-do list of thirty items is setting himself up for anger and frustration at himself and others.

Persons on diets should give themselves reasonable weight-goals or daily calorie counts to achieve. The same goes for any goal-oriented part of our lives. As we reach our goals, we should raise them and continue to challenge ourselves. But we should also be willing to tolerate not reaching a goal when we have done our best. Time and gradual progress are needed for the accomplishment of most worthwhile goals. Christianity does not teach "instant Christian maturity"; but we are admonished to continue striving toward the goal. Struggle and failure are normal steps toward successfully meeting goals.

## Express Anger at Self

Of the two forms of anger expression, venting or suppressing, the burying of anger in prolonged feelings of failure and self-loathing probably does the most harm. Being momentarily mad at oneself for missing a tennis stroke is normal, related as it is only to the failure of the moment. But, if a person allows many frustrating episodes to form a low self-image, the individual may begin to regard himself or herself as a failure. Some outward displays of anger at self, such as muttering to oneself for letting an umbrella get inverted by the wind, are good in that they are honest appraisals of one's own faults. One's inability to honestly admit faults and failures results in turning anger within, and leads to more serious self-image problems. If we have suppressed anger at ourselves, usually we cannot laugh at ourselves, and this ability to laugh at self and accept self in spite of faults is a healthy ingredient to a good self-image.

1. *Keep control, but surrender power.* Damage to self-esteem from insult, humiliation, and ridicule is a very powerful elicitor of anger in people.[8] When our feelings of self-worth are suddenly challenged, we react almost automatically in anger. These feelings temporarily restore good feelings about self, as we have noted, and produce a challenge to the damaging information. This is because anger carries with it a sense of power, strength, and authority.

People with poor self-images are likely to get angry because they tend to attribute hostile intentions to others as the causes

143

of their frustrations.[9] If we possess healthy self-images we can more accurately interpret others' intentions and avoid angry feelings. An example of this type of anger might be when a husband doesn't know where he is driving and his wife suggests that he has made a wrong turn. At this point, he has the opportunity of humbly admitting that they are lost, and thanking her for her observation, or he can strive to preserve self-image by angrily insisting that he knows where he is going. We can almost predict how the husband will react, based on how he views himself, as well as how his wife conveys respect to him.

Healthy self-image is much better supported by humility than by pride. Humility, as we said earlier, provides an accurate view of both one's weaknesses and strengths. But pride can lead us to believe a lie about self. The humble person has enough strength of character and self-worth to admit, "I am lost" or "I need help." With a strong self-image, I can realize that being a good driver or being rich or beautiful are not accurate measures of self-worth.

To avoid the anger of a poor self-image we should counsel people to surrender their pursuit of control and power, and accept themselves for who and what they are.

2. *Fix the blame.* When our counselees think and act from strong self-images, they are ready to stop blaming others and face up to their own imperfections. For some angry people, examining their own imperfections is hazardous because the pain of self-confrontation can lead to denial and the shifting of blame to another person. Others have the opposite problem: They usually do not become angry at anyone, because they see everything that happens to them as their own fault. Their anger is a self-punishing weapon and their need is to learn how to take the pressure off of self and put the blame where it belongs.

A proper expression of anger can be a useful tool in dealing with debilitating guilt feelings. An improper expression, such as that of a woman who remains angry because her father molested her when she was ten years old, fails to solve her anger problem. The chronic pattern of self-blame and guilt feelings in such cases is so common that counselors often encourage strong feelings of anger against the offending party in order to bring self out from under the pile of guilt feelings. Intense anger can diminish these guilt feelings, but the resulting hatred and bitterness is a medicine worse than the disease.

What people need in such cases is to pull themselves away from the shame of what happened and admit that it was not their fault. The problem in the case of the abused girl lies with the father, not the adult woman. In fixing the blame on her father, she can learn to deal constructively with her anger, and can eventually forgive him. People do not have to be enraged to rid themselves of excessive guilt feelings. They need to put blame where it belongs and then strive to forgive themselves or those who hurt them.

It is helpful, in learning how to deal with guilt feelings, to realize that God never intends to use guilt feelings of shame and fear as motivators.[10] What God intends is godly sorrow (2 Cor. 7:10), the feeling that a behavior is so wrong that one must make a change. The motivation to change is not shame or fear of punishment, but the love of God and love for the offended party. Godly sorrow represents an increasing awareness of sin, but a decreasing sense of shameful guilt feelings.

3. *Develop a habit of friendly self-confrontation.* Counselors should help their counselees practice a regular self-analysis, verbalizing to themselves how well they are doing and where they have deviated from their expectations. The goal of such self-confrontation is not to be punishing or threatening to self, but to know themselves well. If self-information comes from situations or people who point out their faults, there is no reason to get angry, because they should not be committed to protecting a perfect view of self. Self-analysis for our counselees means that they admit to strong and weak points in their characters. Knowledge of those weak points does not have to bring shame, but can be a help in avoiding potential problems.

4. *Find a trusted friend.* The process of self-analysis works best if our counselee has a devoted friend or group that can be counted on to tell the person when he or she is wrong or is straying from a righteous path. The atmosphere of love and acceptance a loving friend provides works against a person's tendencies to either become overly critical of self or to ignore faults in a feeling of self-righteousness.[11]

Some Christians have close friends or relatives who can serve in this role, people with whom they can be totally honest and who feel free to confront them. For many of us, a small Bible-study group committed to mutual growth could serve this purpose. I have breakfast once a week with a Christian man I greatly admire. He has a demonstrated Christian maturity and is a few years older and wiser than I. Our times of prayer together are times for discussion of any frustrations we are experiencing in our Christian growth. We meet in an environment of honesty inspired by mutual loving acceptance; and we also expect to be challenged to change and mature. Every Christian, and particularly every Christian leader, ought to have such a confrontive partner to help him or her see what is hard to see about oneself. Regularly we hear of Christian leaders who have fallen in some indiscretion. People can prevent such pitfalls by a knowledge of themselves that produces—not anger and disappointment in self—but a renewed desire to purify themselves.

5. *Accept the truth about yourself.* A healthy self-image is based on an accurate view of self. Our counselees' subjective biases are often so strong that it is difficult for them to have a totally accurate picture of their motives, thoughts, and deeds. The psychological principle of cognitive dissonance suggests that a person finds it very difficult to accept information that is damaging to one's self-concepts. It is easy for some people to see their neighbors as argumentative or pushy, but hard to observe the same in themselves.

The opposite is true in people who are angry at themselves or who possess poor self-images. They tend to overemphasize their failures or other people's statements or actions concerning them, insisting on seeing the negative side just as some people refuse to admit that anything negative is true of themselves. We counselors should work with our counselees to help them rationally evaluate any information about themselves and be prepared to accept the truth, even if it goes against what they expect or desire.

6. *Forgive yourself.* Many great sinners in the Bible found themselves accepted and forgiven by God, much to their surprise. And our counselees are to have the same forgiving

attitude toward themselves. This does not mean that they will not feel terrible remorse at sin and its consequences. But they are not to look at themselves with hate, anger, or loathing. Sin is something terrible, but love is something greater. They have to forget the past and concentrate on the future no matter how many past failures they have.

In learning to forgive themselves they must learn to avoid the countless, self-punishing messages that they might be sending to themselves every day. Each time a woman passes a mirror and looks at her reflection in disapproval she has said something to herself. When a businessman sees piles of undone work, or a mother hears of another mother who leads daily devotionals with her children, they may be telling themselves that they are not measuring up.

When we come into contact with our apparent failures, we need to change the negative messages flashing into our minds. This does not mean ignoring the failure. In fact, we can use the pressure of failure as motivation to do better next time. We can say to ourselves, *I am making progress,* or *there are other areas that demand my attention,* or *this is not a failure and I refuse to compare myself to others.* The last message is very important. Angry people need to stop the comparison-to-others messages and work with themselves the way they are.

# CHAPTER 10

## COUNSELING AND ANGER AT GOD

During times of suffering, anger at God can become a problem even for a committed Christian. But being angry at God is not a subject often addressed in Christian circles, because many think it represents a lack of faith and spiritual maturity. This position is taken even though one book in the Bible portrays a man's anger at God and how it was resolved. The book of Job presents the story of a man angry at God for his undeserved suffering—and Job was angry without sin. Such anger may result from the loss of purpose and the massive doses of fear and helplessness that accompany great personal tragedies.

Pam and Dave experienced the depths of shock and disillusionment when their sixteen-year-old son was killed in an automobile accident. He was their only child. The whole world for Pam and Dave became numb and unreal. They could not believe it was happening to them. Overnight their lives were irrevocably changed. They mobilized their energies during the long days after the public viewing, the funeral, the visits of relatives and friends, and public condolences, but their life was blown away. Going on with life seemed impossible, for life now had no meaning, no purpose.

And yet they had to go on. In one survey of widows, the majority of the bereaved continued in grief for years; most of them did not feel that they had adjusted well even after four years.[1] Grief is an ongoing, lifelong process rather than a crisis to be mastered in a certain period of time.[2]

The energy to go on living has to come from somewhere in the wake of a disaster or tragedy, and anger often fills this energy void, if motivation to continue cannot be found anywhere else. Anger helps the ones suffering by fighting against the feelings of depression and guilt.[3] And anger at God, rather than at some other person, seems the logical direction for painful feelings to travel. Pam and Dave did not want to be angry at God for the death of their only child, but they could not help feeling betrayed. All of the pious reassurances from their Christian friends, and the funeral message on trusting God, reminded them of who could have prevented the tragedy. They felt that God had abandoned them. In the months that followed, both Pam and Dave would have to deal with feelings of anger toward God, an anger so intense that it drained them of joy and negatively impacted their relationship.

Nick and Tammy, and their family of four children, also experienced tragedy. Their youngest daughter, who was three years old, suffered severe brain seizures which left her brain-damaged and severely retarded. No parent is ever prepared for this type of tragedy. Parents plan normal, happy lives for their children. Nick and Tammy were afraid of what was happening and what the future would be like. They had to witness their child's sickness in every detail as it affected all the family, and they felt powerless in the face of what was invading their lives.

Nick was angry—at the doctors, at his family, and at his co-workers. He did not know exactly what to be angry at, but lurking in the back of his mind was the unanswered question: Where was God in all this?

This unanswered question makes it very difficult for suffering people such as Nick and Tammy to listen to Christian teaching about God's being in control, or about his having a purpose in all things. Those who suffer greatly are in a deep emotional sea and their own emotions rise and fall out of control. Depression and anger are two of the most common emotions linked to intense suffering and grief.[4] In times of weakness, anger easily rises up and becomes the silent partner in suffering. Just like any anger that is directed at another person or event, anger at God must be acknowledged and dealt with.

People often use anger to push away painful things that they cannot or will not deal with. This was the case with one character in the film *Children of a Lesser God*. Sarah, who was deaf, refused to learn to speak because she was angry about her past. She had been hurt and rejected and she let her anger and her deafness wall her into a world of silence, free from pain. In order to love a man, Sarah had to expose her anger and pain and risk the feeling of more pain and rejection.

Anger is a way of fighting back, of doing something when people feel most helpless. But the disadvantage of anger is that it does not allow people to come to terms with and accept the misfortune that has occurred in their lives. Our anger during times of emotional or physical suffering is likely to be directed toward people, especially those we depend upon and love. It is difficult to be angry at life, or fate, or a disease. We cannot hurt those things, nor do they give us a hearing. But people can be hurt and will listen.

Anger during times of pain is like a shout of anguished questions that demand a hearing. Other people, especially our loved ones, become the target of suffering anger, because they have to listen. We may become angry at a doctor for not doing more, or we may become irritable with our family because we are hurting. But very often our anger almost unthinkingly finds its path to God because he is a person, one on whom we depend, and because we see him as responsible and silent and having failed to help us in our time of need.

## ANGER WHILE SUFFERING MAY BE IRRATIONAL

People are overwhelmed by disease, or the death of loved ones, the constant pain of arthritis, the prospect of a life of paralysis or blindness, the departure of a wife or husband. Some are hit so hard, so fast, that their reasoning powers are all but paralyzed. The parent whose child is dying of leukemia is not open to reasoned statements of God's purpose, but needs a loving presence, a comforting arm, a listening ear, a handkerchief. A counselor can be there to meet these needs for suffering people.[5]

People could be prepared in advance for suffering by fixing in their minds what they believe about God's love and purposes, his future restoration of all things, and the relationship of pain to growth. Sailors must do this at sea. They batten down the hatches, pull in the sails, and turn the ship into the wind before a storm hits. When the storm of suffering arrives, it consumes the individual's attention; he or she has to ride it out, clinging to the mast. Rational beliefs are very important during these times, but feelings will rise and fall anyway. With time, one's reasoned faith can be recalled and understood more clearly.

The dominance of emotions over reason during times of suffering was seen in the life of C. S. Lewis who wrote a rational answer to the problem of suffering in his book, *The Problem of Pain.*[6] Lewis understood God's universe and the place of suffering in it, and how an all-good and all-powerful God could allow evil and suffering. But when his wife died, he struggled emotionally with the problem of pain in his own life. He expressed his anguish and doubts in journals, and later in another book, *A Grief Observed.*[7] His faith was shaken to its very roots, but not uprooted. His expression of loss and frustration and anger at God in his thoughts and in his journals was very helpful to him in finding his way through the shadow and back to the light of his reasoned faith.

## IS IT RIGHT TO BE ANGRY AT GOD?

Is anger at God a sin? The answer to this question will guide us in working with those who are angry at God. If anger at God is not necessarily sinful, and if such anger can be expressed properly and can serve the communication between God and human beings, then we should be careful before we chastise those who suffer for expressing their honest feelings to God.

In the Bible, God does not forbid or condemn the expression of anger toward him, especially during times of great suffering. In fact, God seems to encourage man's honest outcries of agony. Job may contain the best example in the Bible of God's attitude toward the angry, suffering person. With God's permission Job has lost his wealth, his children, and his health. But he is not a broken man. Yet Job's anger at God is obvious to Bildad, one of his three visitors (Job 18:4, 30:20–21). God did not condemn Job for expressing exactly how he felt toward him. He understood and accepted Job's blunt expression of his hurt and despair. Job could not imagine that God was dealing fairly with him, and he let God know what he thought.

In the book of Jonah, God responds to Jonah's anger, not by punishing him, but by teaching him. Jonah had disagreed with God's decision to spare the city of Nineveh. He said, "I am angry enough to die" (Jonah 4:2–4); nothing God said indicated that he was censoring Jonah's uninhibited expression of his true feelings.

Elijah is another example of an angry biblical character. He was confused, afraid, and appears to have been angry at God for what was happening to him (1 Kings 19). But Elijah was still faithful and obedient.

The common ingredient in these three biblical illustrations is that they were interacting with God in their anger. They believed in God's character, but were confused about how their specific situations related to God's perfect will. They did not lack faith, and thus they did not act with hostility and reject God. It was out of their faith in God that they raised their objections about what was happening.

The counselor should keep this in mind when counseling suffering people. Doubts are not equivalent to a lack of faith. People have doubts because the reasoned beliefs they cherish are being challenged and they need to rise to meet the challenge. Doubts and questions and attempts to understand are evidences of some faith in God. Because people believe something about

God's character and depend on him they may feel the emotional arousal of anger at God. It is not a sin if that anger leads counselees to question God and to attempt to understand his actions. If, on the other hand, people are using their anger to reject God's purpose and plan, their anger expression is sin.

## THE PURPOSE OF EXPRESSING ANGER TO GOD

Anger does not appear at first glance to be a godly, Christian emotion one should express toward God. How can it be good or serve any purpose? In answering this question, remember that anger feelings themselves are not a sin, but it is only in the expression of anger in thoughts or behaviors that sin may occur. Anger is a legitimate emotion, experienced even by God, and it does have its purposes in people's relationships with God.

Since God already knows the thoughts and feelings of suffering people, the purpose that an honest expression of anger to God might serve is primarily for their benefit and not for his information. Expressing their anger and honest feelings before God moves the anger out where it can be acknowledged, analyzed, and dealt with. Expression that is proper and constructive should lend structure to very vague but negative feelings and allow them to be compared with what is known about God, his character, and his purposes.

Emotions that are not expressed in spoken or written words do not exist in a form that can be easily understood, challenged, or compared with other knowledge. Emotions are vague feelings that may lead to specific, habitual behaviors without careful thought about the matter. Verbally expressed emotions, on the other hand, are the result of people's thoughts interacting with their feelings.

Anger at God can be expressed in the counselor's office. Such expression not only gives people the feeling that they have been heard and understood by the almighty God, but also serves with a counselor's aid to help people see from God's perspective how tragedy exists in a larger scheme of things.

For example, Job did not learn the purpose for his suffering, but he was satisfied after his encounter with God because his outcry was heard. God convinced Job of his almighty knowledge and power and care for the world, and Job realized that his tragedy was surely not a situation that had somehow escaped God's interest or grasp. Job talked angrily with God and came away with a stronger faith in who God is. Job suffered. He expressed his anger to God. He saw who God was. He submitted to God's will. The same thing can happen to people who are angry at God when counselors help them express this anger.

## How Should Suffering People Pray?

My mother, who has suffered many years from multiple sclerosis, asked me once if she should pray to God for healing. We discussed biblical examples that show that a person should feel free to express to God exactly what is felt or wanted. We concluded that a person may cry out to God for life, or to be free of cancer, or to have children back. Then, after some time perhaps, he or she should tell God in faith that what is really wanted (even though it is not felt) is God's will. This is the prayer to pray because his will is best. This is a hard thing to do, but it is faith.

Job, who listened to God remind him of who he is and of what power and knowledge he has, showed no more anger at God (Job 38–42). He was satisfied by what he knew of God. The anger subsided and Job's life went on from there.

Jesus, in the Garden of Gethsemane, prayed that the hour of his death and separation from his Father would pass, but he immediately added, "Yet not as I will, but as you will" (Matt. 26:39). In the garden Jesus was in agony to the point of a bloody sweat. However, after he expressed his will to God, and that he wanted God's will, his emotions were relieved and he calmly let the soldiers take him to his death. Our counselees' emotions of anger and fear and helplessness may not disappear as rapidly as the Son of God's. But, if we help them make honest expressions of anger to God and submit to his love and power, they will find some relief in their troubles. This is easy to say, but not easy to do: People who are angry at God need to submit to God's will. This submission during times of suffering is not easy, but it is possible through a clear expression of anger and an attempt to see things from his perspective.

## LIMITATIONS OF ANGER TOWARD GOD

When the counselor helps people express their anger and hurt openly before God and focus on who God is, then they can begin to see how great God's love and wisdom is for them. Such a change requires that people remove themselves from the pride of their own case against God and submit to his perfect will. Suffering people do not have to cease feeling pain; they only need to abandon the sin of rejecting God who has allowed them to hurt. It would not be right or helpful for counselees to unleash their anger feelings toward God defiantly or hatefully. This type of anger expression demonstrates rebellion and the pride of saying they know more than God. People should express their anger feelings and then try to understand and accept what God is doing.

Anger expression during times of suffering is not constructive or proper unless we keep in mind that the expression of anger should ultimately help us find peace and submission within God's will. Peace will not come by merely the expression of anger to God. But if we attempt to be open to what we learn from his perspective, we will know peace.

God speaks to suffering people through his Word, through other Christians, in the silent moments of prayer, through professional counselors—but we must be willing to listen.

When our counselees are honestly angry with God, and they are hurt and cannot seem to believe any more, they are not rejecting God. Even in such anger, people can ask God for comfort or for a change in the situation. They are still letting God be God, which is the basis for faith. The motive of expressing anger before God must be to find relief from the pain and to end any negative feelings that exist toward him. Our counselees need to believe God is still there and still cares when they have been hurt. Unbelieving anger is an attempt to break the relationship with God, merely because people have been hurt or because they wish to seal themselves in silence and prevent more pain in this God-controlled world.

God understands these feelings and wants suffering people to bring them to him. We need to encourage those who suffer to continue to be open to the possibility that God loves and God knows what he is doing. Tell them not to give up. Hate will not make the pain go away; it only sidetracks and numbs people. Real living is coming to the truth about what is going on in the universe and living in league with God's plan to eventually heal all. But such a response is difficult, and we must be patient—even if it takes years to resolve anger toward God.

Rejecting God will not change the nature of the world. Suffering and death still await everyone. Anger and hate provide only ineffective, numbing shields to these life-shattering events. To not give in to hate and to express anger feelings to God is an attempt to accept the world as it is; and it is our only hope to find peace of mind in hospitals, wheelchairs, funerals, and lonely bedrooms.

### THINK THROUGH THE PROBLEM OF SUFFERING

At some point, all anger, even anger at God, has to be confronted by rational thought. The time, though, for the counselor to engage in a reasoned discussion of suffering is not while a person is in the throes of emotional pain. Someone who has just lost a son in a car accident does not need to hear about why God allows suffering. That person needs to be surrounded by people who care. Eventually, however, reasons for God's actions and the nature of the spiritual world in which we live have to be understood by the suffering individual. The counseling session can be an effective place and time for this.

We need an explanation that will explain how "bad things" that happen to us could exist in God's world. Our hearts find emotional peace, not just from the emotional release of caring friends or busy distractions, but also and ultimately from a belief system that makes sense and satisfies our aching hearts. In the following pages I want to discuss, in a preliminary way, some questions the counselor may encounter. Further reading is recommended so the counselor may be fully prepared.

1. *Why didn't God create good people?* If God had created morally good people, incapable of sin, there would have been no Fall, and no death or suffering say some skeptics. God could have created "good" robots, but not good people—persons

with the freedom to choose good or evil. Without this freedom, people aren't people.

It is also important to realize that God not only created Adam and Eve with freedom to choose; he also created them in the middle of Satan's rebellion. God knew of the possibility of the Fall and the consequent human struggle. His plan included placing Adam and Eve in dangerous circumstances, which resulted in all the suffering and evil we experience. Our counselees must see God, not as making a bad mistake, but as having a plan larger than they can see.

2. *Wouldn't it have been better if God had never created people?* When great suffering overtakes people, they are tempted to wish they had never been born. But how could it be better for them if they had never been created? We can only speculate: would it have been better for God if we had never been created to face suffering? But, obviously, God did decide to create human beings and his plan included a plan of salvation to restore us and deliver us from potential suffering.

3. *Why doesn't God eliminate all the evil people in the world?* If God did this, then no one would be left, because everyone has committed acts of evil or has hurt someone else. All are sinners! Why should God wipe out the Hitlers of the world and not ordinary people who have gotten angry? God does not rank sins. All sin is evil. If he is not going to tolerate sin, then everyone must die.

4. *Why doesn't an all-powerful God intercept all the consequences of evil in the world?* God could stop falling boulders, eliminate cancer cells, and evaporate the robber's gun. Everyone speaking unkind words would become temporarily mute. Anyone who lusted would become temporarily blind.

This may sound good, but it would leave the world in total chaos. Any action with any potential negative consequences would be stopped. Nasty thoughts could be dealt with by temporarily rendering the thinker unconscious. Think of such a world where all evil is stopped by God. The whole world would either be unconscious or deaf, dumb, and blind. No such world is possible.

If people are to exist, freedom to sin or to obey, must be a part of it, along with all the possible suffering that sin causes. The fact that God created man as he did, when he could have chosen not to do so, should make us wonder what great plan he has that is so important to make all this suffering worth it.

5. *Why doesn't God stop this specific suffering in my life?* This is a good question that people may raise before God. Why does he allow this person's son to die, or cancer to strike this child, or this great earthquake to occur? Why is there so much suffering and an apparent uneven distribution of it?

The problem with people who are angry at God is that they doubt his character, particularly his love and wisdom in caring for them. But it is neither fair nor rational of us to doubt God's character the way an atheist doubts God's existence. It may sound wise to taunt, but the whole drama of God's Creation, man's Fall, and God's plan of salvation is not that simple. Nor is all of it revealed to us. God chose to create free human beings as the highest, most noble creatures in his universe. The seventy years or so we live are only a minute fraction of eternity; and they are a prologue to the rest of eternity. We need a larger perspective in times of suffering, even though physical or emotional pain focuses our attention only on ourselves and our personal agony.

As counselors, we do not know why God doesn't spare a child's life or deliver a loved one from cancer. But we do know he wants us to trust him with our lives and our futures, and to trust that he knows what he is doing. While we do not see all of God's great plan, certain truths are made very clear in the Bible in the person of Jesus Christ. Jesus was all-powerful. He could even raise the dead from the grave. He had power over death and suffering, and he used it. In addition, Jesus was and still is the world's perfect example of the all-loving God. He was moved with compassion over the human condition. He fed the five thousand people because he had compassion on them. He wept at Lazarus's grave because of the whole drama of death affecting human beings.

Jesus had the power and the love, yet he did not heal everyone. God did not end the satanic rebellion, but created Adam and Eve in Satan's stronghold and told them to rule. Suffering and death became a near certainty at that moment, but God deemed it better to let man act in his place than to save man the pain, and he knew he would resolve the problem of evil in the end.

The Bible does not give us every reason for man's suffering, but it does say that suffering can produce a greater good in people. According to the Bible, suffering can refine our faith (1 Pet. 2:5–7), allow us an opportunity to show the works of God (John 9:1–3), conform us to Christ's image (Rom. 8:28–29), produce in us perseverance and character (Rom. 5:3–5), and make us mature (James 1:2–4). Consider James 1:2–4 in The Living Bible translation:

> Is your life full of difficulties and temptations? Then be happy, for when the way is rough, your patience has a chance to grow. So let it grow, and don't try to squirm out of your problems. For when your patience is finally in full bloom, then you will be ready for anything, strong in character, full and complete.

Our counselees must not fall into the emotional trap of seeing all suffering as planned by God to mature their characters. This is certainly not true in Job's case, an outstanding example of God's use of tribulation. Job was a man of godly character, and there is no indication that his suffering was for the purpose of his growth. Some suffering can obviously be used by God to mature character, while other suffering bears no relationship to character development. In all cases suffering people must trust in God.

To teach that all pain is designed by God to produce spiritual maturity could leave parents holding their dead child in their arms, angrily asking God, "Could you not have matured my character in some less drastic way?" Rabbi Harold Kushner, who does not accept the benefit of New Testament revelation, wrote the book *When Bad Things Happen to Good People.*[8] He said that God cannot stop suffering rather than declare that God is in control and has his reasons. Philip Yancey argues convincingly for this latter position saying that it better fits the New Testament revelation of Christ.[9]

159

If we believe God is in control and that he has some unspoken reason for allowing our suffering, of course it is much easier to be angry with him. But we can only lose if we persist in that. Those who surrender to God's power and trust him to show his goodness do attest to God's loving and merciful work, and the Bible further shows us—when we do not know this in our own limited experience—that he can be trusted with what we do not see. God is not a God who has no power over evil and suffering; he is a God of wisdom and love, and Job had to trust him (Job 38–40). Through much emotional turmoil Job found satisfaction in this answer. And so can the hurt, angry people we counsel.

### COUNSELORS SHOULD LISTEN

We need to listen to a person's anger without necessarily agreeing with that person's hostility toward God. Job's friends were not the best companions he could have had during his suffering, but they were not the worst either. Many Christians choose to avoid the suffering person who is angry and cannot praise God. We can be *there* for the angry man or woman, and we can listen.

What angry people need initially is not a lesson on the sinfulness of anger, but one's love and presence. They need to feel that they are not alone and that people understand what they are going through. Nothing is more reassuring than the presence of a policeman or a doctor when people have been in a serious automobile accident. The presence of such a person helps stabilize people's fears and sense of helplessness. The same feelings are projected toward counselors and loved ones who stand with suffering people when they go through great tragedy, even if it appears that nothing can be done to help.

### COUNSELORS SHOULD DEAL WITH THE ANGER

If people are having difficulty getting over their anger, then counseling should begin to explore the reasons for the anger and ways of dealing with it properly. The individual may need to deal with a loss of security due to the tragedy, or self-pity, or the larger perspectives—the context within which the suffering is occurring. The counselor has first been present with the sufferer and offered hope and reassurance; he or she has offered an arm to lean on, and has listened to the cry of anger and pain. Then, as the angry person is feeling less helpless and alone, the counselor can begin to help him or her see and accept the suffering in the context of biblical reality. There is no avoiding this last task. Sooner or later, bitterness and anger at life—and at God—have to be dealt with by accepting life as it is. The biblical answer to anger at God is to accept God's agenda and perspective on reality. Fortunately, he loves people more than they love themselves and such a step of faith is possible.

## ACCEPTING ONE'S LOT IN LIFE

Catastrophic loss robs people of meaning and purpose and leaves them either angry or emptied of spirit, hollow and beaten by life. Often, anger at God or the tragedy itself keeps people from dissolving into meaninglessness. But such anger, while it keeps the spirit alive, will kill the spirit eventually, since it can only isolate them in their pain, and not bestow understanding or hope.

Ecclesiastes speaks of how to have meaning in life in spite of suffering by trusting in God who is in control. The book teaches us to see our lives as in his sovereign plan. Instead of being an endless cycle of chance—which is one description of life "under the sun" (1:3), life "under heaven" (3:1) is seen as ordered. This truth is imaged in the poetry of Ecclesiastes 3:1–8, which says there is a time for everything, both the good and the bad. Meaning does not come to Christians because they have no suffering, but because the world is controlled by God. This is one's lot in life, and there is security, not in freedom from pain, but in knowing that nothing is out of his control. To have cancer is not suddenly to lose security and hope or be betrayed by God. Cancer is reason enough for fear and anguish, but it is not reason for anger at God or loss of meaning in life.

How we express that anger depends upon what or who the object of our anger is. It serves no purpose to get angry at a flat tire. Nothing can be accomplished by kicking it. We must hold back the anger and deal with it. Anger at another human being is a different matter. We must be slow to anger, but then, by expressing anger properly, we can work on the relationship in ways that protect us from hurt while allowing the relationship to mature. Anger at God affects our counselees' most important relationship. They should not be afraid to expose that anger to God, who is ultimately responsible for all things in their lives. When they express their pain to God properly, they are expressing trust in him, and their walk with him will deepen.

# CHAPTER ELEVEN

# PREVENTING ANGER

Imagine anger in the life of a good Christian pastor. Tom is late for work and becomes irritated with his children, but he controls his temper. He constructively corrects their misbehavior. Then, a few minutes before he leaves for work, he loses his temper at his wife, who has obviously been giving him the silent treatment. It frustrates him that every time she has a grievance with him she brings it up just five minutes before he has to leave for work. But, he apologizes for being angry with her and promises that they will talk about it later that evening.

When his car stalls on the freeway, Tom becomes mad and slams his hand on the steering wheel. Then, realizing that being late for work will not cause any problems, he takes several deep breaths and tries to start the car again. It eventually starts, but he is still a little angry over the fact that he will have to take time later to get the car to a mechanic. But, he keeps telling himself that there are bigger problems in the world than his.

Once at work Tom is still irritated about his car. His assistant pastor sees him and comments sarcastically, "I suppose head pastors can be late for work when they want to." His assistant has always seemed sarcastic to him, and though he knows it is because of the man's poor self-image, he is angered nonetheless. He had recently requested this assistant keep more regular office hours.

He does not respond to the assistant's words, but merely walks into his own office. He knows he should not let things bother him; therefore, Tom goes later into the assistant pastor's office just to visit and have a cup of coffee with him. Tom does not want to allow a bad relationship to develop between him and his assistant.

This pastor responded properly to each of the anger situations in which he found himself. And his good responses were helping him defeat the anger habit. He may be doing well in learning to handle his anger, but imagine how much more pleasant his life would be and how much more impact he would have on others if he did not often become angry. The peace of not getting angry is the goal of anger prevention. But such peace is not possible if people are constantly reacting in anger to life's "bad weather."

When I talk about preventing anger, I am not talking about just another counseling technique, but an approach that stresses a change of character and a maturing in the fruit of the Spirit. James and John were called the "sons of thunder" (Mark 3:17); we might more literally say, "sons of anger." John was prone to anger early in his life. He interrupted Christ's teaching on humility (Luke 9:46–50); he wanted Christ to rain fire down on a Samaritan village (Luke 9:51–53); and he wanted power over the other disciples in Christ's future kingdom (Mark 10:35–40). But in time John was transformed into the man who wrote so eloquently on Christian love (1 John).

The Bible gives strong warnings about avoiding anger, because its consequences are so damaging. Anger can devour us. It can steal our joy and ministry with others. Proverbs 25:28 warns that, "Like a city whose walls are broken down is a man who lacks self-control." We can be angry and deal with it properly, but to be constantly angry leaves us emotionally drained and vulnerable to sin. Maturity is peace, patience, and self-control. "A man's wisdom gives him patience; it is to his glory to overlook an offense" (Proverbs 19:11).

## NOT GETTING ANGRY—AND SOLVING A PROBLEM

If anyone had a reason to be angry, Jenny did. She experienced a problem over several years of her life that challenged her emotions and her Christian faith to their limits. She solved her problem and avoided bitterness and possible emotional problems, by avoiding anger during a three-year emotional ordeal.

Jenny's problem was with her best friend's father. He was continually making sexual advances toward her. This attention had started gradually—just a friendly touch, a small present—but eventually he was touching her where he should not and even forced her to kiss him once. She was frightened and too ashamed to tell anyone. To complicate matters the man was an outstanding leader in her church of which her father was the pastor.

When Jenny went away to college, she thought her problem was over; but whenever she returned home and to her church, the man would approach her and try to catch her alone. Knowing she had to do something, Jenny saw a counselor, who convinced her that she had to tell her parents, which she did. After much questioning, they were convinced that their daughter was innocent and that the man might be a threat to his own daughters or to young girls in the church.

When Jenny's father confronted the man, he denied the charges and set out to convince others in the church that the pastor's family was persecuting him. Jenny's best friend was bitter and said she hated her. Jenny's father eventually resigned from the church rather than split the church on this issue. The man who had sexually harassed Jenny was never confronted by his church or family although Jenny suspected that his wife knew of his problem.

Through all of this emotional turmoil Jenny and her family survived because they refused to give in to anger and hate. Jenny may not have been experienced enough to know how to deal with sexual harassment, but she was mature enough to not give in to resentment and hate. She did not use anger to hide her shame or her lack of power to stop the man. He knew she would not tell her dad without stirring up problems. Jenny felt sorry for the man, but did not hate him. She had just enough righteous anger to stop this man from hurting any other young girls. She loved her best friend and understood her reaction, even when the friend rejected her.

Jenny did not descend into anger at herself, because she knew she was innocent. She did not become angry at God for what had happened to her even though she and her family were bound to be hurt, no matter what she did. She did not get angry at her parents when they struggled with doing the right thing by their daughter. Jenny was not left emotionally un-scarred by these events; in fact, she suffered fear, guilt, shame, and depression. Her ability to relate to young men at college was also affected. But anger would have only compounded her problem and deepened the emotional scars. Jenny recovered because she was eventually able to forgive and get on with her life.

Jenny's sense of peace in not being angry was not an emotion-less, zombie-like state; it was more akin to being in the eye of a hurricane. Fears and doubts swirled around her, but in spite of everything she still had hope that this problem would be resolved.

Acquiring the freedom to not get angry takes a lot of work. Being peaceful is not just learning to bite one's tongue; it is learning to not get angry or hold grudges. Most of the time anger responses are the opposite of the fruit of the Spirit. Anger is not love, joy, peace, patience, kindness, goodness, gentleness, faithfulness, or self-control (Gal. 5:22–23).

Most people with anger problems do not consider anger their problem. They usually think of the situation or the person with whom they are angry as the problem, not their anger.

Also, people do not usually seek out counselors to calm their tempers. They seek counseling to save their marriages or to end their depressions; only later does the counselor convince them to work on their anger problems.

Therefore, to prevent anger people have to sincerely want to be mature and grow in the image of Christ. They have to desire the freedom to not get angry, the power to not be bitter, and the ability to control their words and actions. That power, that control, and that maturity represent the goal of anger prevention.

## ANGER PREVENTION STARTS IN THE MIND

Anger is a combination of emotional arousal, thoughts, and actions. Preventing anger does not mean becoming an emotionless person. The key to the human personality is not in human feelings, or behaviors, or even in the thoughts alone, but in the mind's interaction with feelings and behaviors. Frustration feelings are normal when people are misunderstood or lonely, but how they will experience these feelings depends upon their mind-set. Each of our minds is deeply ribbed with beliefs that sift every developing feeling and thought, and give rise to the commands and energies of behavior. It is in the mind that anger, as a sinful thought or behavior, must be transformed. Notice, I did not say "stopped"—the mind is no wall.

The mind is the source of character, where new feelings are shaped into emotions. Raw frustration, bitter memories, physical injury, sudden surprise, fears, and hostile conversation must all be grabbed and absorbed by the mind's beliefs, expectations, attitudes, and commitments. With an angry mind-set, feelings become twisted into resentment and rage. With better, more positive beliefs and commitments, the raw hostile feelings are intercepted and confronted. But with a perfect mind-set, peace can dominate the heart.

### Having a Biblical Mind-set

Basic to the attitude that stimulates peace, as opposed to anger, is a knowledge of life's true purpose. Christians believe in a God of wisdom, fairness, and justice. We believe that evil and suffering are present for a time because of the Fall. Many Christians give mere intellectual assent to these and other theistic beliefs, and as a result their Christianity has no impact on their lives. But, those who conscientiously and repeatedly remind themselves of the fact that they live in a God-controlled world, and remind themselves of their purpose to mature in Christlikeness, will react differently to a missed airplane connection, or being insulted, or getting old.

Life is not made serene because people are able to buy their own planes, vanquish their enemies, or dye their gray hair. To avoid anger, people must make conscious, intentional commitments to accept God's lot for themselves, to consider others as worthy of their service, and to see their own growth in Christ as the primary goal in life. They need to make frequent, intentional commitments to not be controlled by anger, but to experience life's frustrations in the context of a belief in God's control, planning, and love.

Counselors should help people see that emotions are a good and normal part of life, but not the essential guide to behavior. Righteous actions, not good feelings, are a biblical priority in life. Therefore, the Bible urges people to give their highest priority to loving others, not to seeing to their own comfort or security. Anger feelings are normal, understandable results of living, but, with rare exceptions, they should not guide the behaviors of life.

Focusing on having good feelings as opposed to exhibiting good behaviors often leads to anger feelings. And then angry thoughts and behaviors are not far behind. The more people have been made aware of and live by beliefs based on spiritual reality and the true purpose in life, the more unconsciously and naturally they become directed by this frame of mind.

Without a deeply ingrained belief system, the development of anger feelings, thoughts, and behaviors is dictated by the fluctuating thoughts and feelings that arise in the presence of flat tires and insults. For a man to promise God that he will never get angry is only minimally effective during times of great stress, because his active, conscious, mental states are wiped clean by a stream of stressful events. Suddenly, un-Christian thoughts and feelings can be guiding his behaviors.

Provoking events and anger feelings have to be met by a

thoughtful, tried-and-proven mind-set that says, *My first responsibility is to love my neighbor. This too will pass. God is in control. I cannot secure my life; only God can do that.*

Anger will not be stopped in its tracks by merely reciting a Bible verse unless that verse is at the top of a mountain of belief. Such beliefs cannot be developed in the heat of the stressful situation, but have to be fixed and formed over the progress of a life committed to Christ.

We have to develop a mind-set that allows us to pursue good moral things—beauty, friendship, affirmation, safety, comfort, rest, morality, respect, job, security, and other things—without clinging to these things and without demanding these things. Secular therapies often recommend similar moral training for the prevention of anger.[1] The biblical mind-set teaches us that people must cling to God and take the things he permits, realizing that nothing in this life is for keeps. It is a paradox. People are most secure when they realize their insecurity in life and find their security in God's promises. With this mind-set, anger can be controlled. But this is not security in Bible verses; it is a firm belief in the way things really are in spite of irritating distractions and suffering.

## Practical Steps in Anger Prevention

Anger prevention occurs, not in religious settings removed from problems, but in the real world of actual and potential anger and hostility. The change from being a person of war to being a person of peace may begin in the commitment one makes in a religious setting. But the path to peace lies through noisy days of irritation, provocation or embarrassment, and the shaping of one's mind to meet affront with love, and irritation with patience. The following are suggestions for counselors to use in guiding people through active steps to the place that anger does not characterize their lives.

1. *Avoid anger-causing situations that you are not yet prepared to handle.* In the past, our counselees have encountered situations in which they have not been able to control their anger. They must learn to avoid such situations and people until they develop the confidence, wisdom, and patience

to handle them. In those areas where they have gotten angry in the past, they should be doubly cautious because they have probably developed a habit of stimulus-anger response.[2]

A businessman who can get along with almost anyone has endured bad confrontations with a man in his company for years. "He's got something against me and I don't know what," he says. "I've tried to relate to him, but nothing worked. He's always pushing me." To stay away from this antagonist is not running away from a problem, but preventing it. He is learning to pray for his antagonist and for his own ability to remain calm when their paths must cross.

2. *Avoid emotional overload.* Our counselees must also guard themselves during times of emotional weakness.

When we are feeling depressed, defeated, afraid, or even very happy, we are susceptible to anger. Knowing this, we counselors should help people recognize the early signs of anger and assist them in developing healthy responses through rehearsal during the counseling session.[3]

3. *Don't neglect your health or proper comfort.* Irritations will come our way, but your ability to handle them may be dictated by the degree to which you possess a whole and healthy body and mind. Exercise, good diet, rest, and entertainment help our bodies respond better to stress. There is wisdom in obtaining proper physical comfort when the alternative is irritating heat, hunger, or injury.

Most of us can get angry on a vacation when we are in a cramped space, like an automobile, with small children for a long while. This should remind us to tell clients to take care of themselves and not to let anger gain a foothold simply because they are tired. If a person is always irritable at the end of the day, teach him or her to change routines and allow time for a snack, or for sitting and reading.

4. *Guard your self-esteem.* Very few personal characteristics will protect a person better against becoming angry than a comfortable, secure feeling about oneself. Counselors should help people accept their weaknesses and do what they can to progress and change. But change takes time. Every day our counselees need to remind themselves of the truth about themselves; for example, that they are valued by God in spite

of their problems. Especially when entering a situation in which he or she is prone to become angry, the person needs the habit of challenging every internal message that heightens one's sense of inadequacy or inability. We should make it our aim to help a counselee learn to listen to criticism without automatically becoming angry and critical of self. Other people's criticism can be in error; but if it is not, then the person should use the information to improve oneself in some way. We have discussed this in more detail in chapter 5, in "Challenging Irrational Beliefs."

5. *Watch your tongue.* The Bible has much to say about the tongue, because it has the ability to carry the mind close to the brink of anger. The tongue, often a weapon of anger, can instantly enrage others. If people learn to guard their words, they give other people's anger a chance to dissipate.

The other half of not speaking is listening. Teach the person to listen to angry people and to evaluate what they are saying. I suggest to a client that he or she ask silently, what is the cause of this person's anger? I counsel them to think of the other person as being worthy of respect, but as having a difficult time.

Further, tell counselees when they are angry or are around angry people, to speak slowly, softly, and kindly.[4] For each instance when they think they should have said something, there are many times when they should have remained silent.

6. *Cultivate honesty in communication.* Suppressed anger seems to build up, and later blow up because when people feel they are not being heard or taken seriously, they use anger to get attention and to communicate their complaint. If, however, communication between people could be constant and honest, there would be far less reason for anger. Even painful things can be shared with care and love.[5]

In the Sermon on the Mount, when Jesus spoke against swearing by an oath (Matt. 5:33–37), he was not giving a commandment against taking an oath in court; he was speaking against lying. Apparently some people, then as now, feel obligated to tell the truth only when under oath. Jesus told his listeners, and us today, to be honest. A person should use common sense and graciousness, of course; there are times to keep

*171*

silent. But if we are honest there will be less of a chance for anger to fester.

7. *Resist competitiveness.* Encourage counselees not to look at life as competition with anyone else. Life is not a race to be better than others in order to feel good about oneself. The more we react with feelings of inadequacy and resentment to those who have greater abilities than ourselves, the more we are setting ourselves on a course of disappointment in life.

Without degrading ourselves, we should think of others as better than ourselves in some way, for indeed, every person has special talents and a unique personality. We should rejoice in others' successes. But we should not try to be anyone else but ourselves. Our task is to help counselees be as good as they can be at whatever tasks and with whatever abilities the Lord has given them. They should not harbor thoughts of anger at life and others, because they cannot always know the meaning behind what happens.

8. *Rid yourself of old angers.* Old resentments that have not been resolved keep us angry. We cannot easily be angry at one thing and peaceful about everything else. If we get angry at others at work, when we go home we may talk about the incident very angrily. We are not angry at our family, but it does not take much for the anger we've experienced at work to be transferred to the members of our families.

Past buried resentments also affect people's daily lives in many ways; they may give us a propensity to more resentment and rage.[6] Having been angry in the past is not the problem, but choosing to remain angry is. A woman who resents her father for never having spent time with his children can have great difficulty relating to her husband whenever he shows a similar fault. Her past resentment makes her more likely to feel angry toward her husband. She must resolve the anger she felt toward her father, at least in her mind, and any guilt feelings associated with it.

9. *Work on current relationships.* Tomorrow's problems often start today. Bitter arguments and a parent's anger with a sixteen-year-old do not start simply because of hair style. They begin when children are young, when the parents are responsible for shaping their children's relationships with their parents.

They begin with the parents' styles of communicating, loving, forgiving, and getting angry. Whether we want to or not, we are always sowing the seeds for our future characters and the kind of relationships we will have.

Our counselees should not despair about the future while looking at present problems; but they should take seriously the fact of the present's influence on the future, and hope that they can change things a little every day. They do not have to be locked into bitterness and bad relationships.

## THE ROLE OF THE CHURCH IN PREVENTING ANGER

One thing that is clear in Scripture is that people do not have to struggle alone. When Christ ascended into heaven, he sent the Holy Spirit to indwell human beings and transform them into creatures after his image. Since Christians share God's life as his children and are indwelt by the Holy Spirit, they are members of the body of Christ.

God's plan is that a person's kinship in the body of Christ gives that one the resources to overcome problems and to reach maturity in Christ. The help God gives to his children is spiritual, but it is not magical. It includes the pastor's teachings from the Bible on problems—such as anger—which face the Christian. Churches also offer the individual valued resources of spiritual maturity. More mature members can assist one who needs help with personal problems. Having a prayer partner, for example, can provide the confrontation and support which a person requires, as well as a healthy personal relationship that can support one's emotional health.

### The Pulpit and Anger Prevention

The pastor in the pulpit has the opportunity to present biblical truth on a variety of issues that are pertinent in helping people. Pastors can build people's knowledge and add to their personal store of what the Bible teaches about marriage and family, discipline in the home, freedom from guilt, and dealing with anger. The Sunday sermon is not sufficient of itself to adequately deal with these topics, but the church can augment a series of Sunday messages with sound teaching in the Sunday school and with recommended books and tapes.

Any teaching on the "musts" of Christian behavior ought to be developed the way Scripture presents them. The New Testament, particularly the Epistles, in dealing with behavior expected of Christians, precedes that with teaching concerning the new nature in Christ and freedom in grace. Any expectation of the Christian life, such as being rid of anger, is seen as the result of one's new life in Christ, and not as a requirement for salvation.

Teaching the truth about anger will not, by itself, change people's lives. They may listen and understand teaching on being slow to anger, but not know how to change. Application of biblical principles must also be a part of the church's focus.

### A Prayer Partner

As Christians we need people in our lives who will listen, confront, counsel, and be constant encouragers. In our journey toward spiritual maturity in Christ, we want partners who will understand us, affirm our worth, and warn us when we are angry. We should ask God for prayer partners with whom we can share mutual responsibility for one another's spiritual growth before the presence of God.

Prayer partners provide accountability we do not have when we struggle alone against anger, or any other problem. With partners a problem can be described and prayed for, and a specific plan of action settled upon. For example, I might plan to pray each day for the people at work whom I have something against. At the end of the week, my prayer partners should ask me how I got along. I'm accountable to prayer partners for specific steps in defeating my anger. Such accountability guards us against sin and contributes to personal growth. Proverbs 27:9 praises the friend who is your counselor. " . . . the pleasantness of one's friend springs from his earnest counsel."

### RIGHTEOUS ANGER

When a person has learned to prevent anger and has grown significantly toward the maturity of inner peace as promised in the fruit of the Spirit and described in the Beatitudes (Gal. 5:22–23; Matt. 5:3–11), he or she is prepared to express righteous anger. Righteous anger comes from a heart of peace and courage. Therefore, it represents one of the highest ingredients of the mature Christian personality. Righteous anger is not merely "blowing one's top" about someone's sin, but is an exhibition of courage and virtue in the face of evil. As much as in any previous period of history, the world now needs some righteously angry Christians who can stand up to evil. God made anger a natural response in human emotions; but very seldom are people prepared to express righteous anger. Only the person who has mastered anger is prepared to express it.

In the Bible, anger is considered righteous if it is directed at evil and is expressed under control. It is anger at the consequences of sin, not a tantrum for failing to get one's way. Jesus expressed righteous anger in Mark 3:5 at the wrongs of the Pharisees. His anger was under control and he used it as a reprimand when, "he looked around at them in anger."

Pastors may find a similar use of righteous anger when they see a need to firmly confront a sinner who is hurting others and is not repentant. Such anger may even be a tool to bring the sinner to repentance. A parent's anger at a child may be righteous, if the anger carries the message of how serious the parent views the child's behavior. The response of a parent who is righteously angry may be similar to that of a child's, who is unrighteously angry, but the cognitive and behavioral expressions of each will be different.

Righteous anger never seeks vengeance, because that is God's right alone. And righteous anger is always bounded by mercy. God's command to love is not negated just because you or I may have righteous anger. The righteous anger of God in the Old Testament is always tempered by his love and mercy and patience.

Anger can be a great motivation for change or defense in the face of overpowering odds. Jesus used anger in his great zeal for his Father's house (John 2:13–17). He directed his anger publicly at a religious system that was hardened and unresponsive even to the teachings and miracles of the Messiah.

A Christian student in a secular college might find a similar use of righteous anger in the presence of nonbelieving professors, who choose to make their classes podiums for attacks on or ridicule of Christianity or a student's personal faith in Christ. A college classroom should be a place where all viewpoints can be heard. But, professors can pursue their own positions in order to antagonize students. Properly expressed, a student's anger in support of the truth can be a tool that will protect that student's rights and gain a fair hearing.

In such a case, the Christian student must consider whether to express his or her anger in the classroom before other students or privately with the professor. Righteous anger is never an easy path.

In most cases, righteous anger demands courage. The person who is prepared to express righteous anger must be a person of peace and patience, one who possesses some of the supernatural wisdom that a mind renewed by Christ can give. There is nothing wrong with the arousal feelings of anger, but unfortunately, much of human anger with its outbursts and resentments is sin. This world of sin and broken relationships needs so much more than outraged hot heads or the teeth gnashing of resentment and bitterness.

Anger does not exist in discomfort or misfortune or in body chemistry, but in people, in their decisions and thoughts and actions. So, too, the control of anger must come from people, from decisions made and followed through and from good counseling. Anger control means being aware of our choice in the midst of stress. It means being willing to not react, to let certain indignities pass, as well as having the courage and wisdom to stand up against other indignities. Then Christian peace rings true: "Get rid of all bitterness, rage and anger. . . . Be kind and compassionate to one another, forgiving each other, just as in Christ God forgave you" (Eph. 4:31–32 NIV).

# BIBLIOGRAPHY

The following sources are recommended reading for the counseling of anger.

Adams, Jay E. *You Can Defeat Anger.* (Grand Rapids, Mich.: Baker Book House), 1975.

Alschuler, Cathryn F., and Alschuler, Alfred S. "Developing Healthy Responses to Anger: The Counselor's Role," *Journal of Counseling and Development* 63 (September 1984): 26–29.

Augsburger, David W. *Anger and Assertiveness in Pastoral Care.* (Philadelphia: Fortress Press), 1979.

Berkowitz, Leonard. "The Case For Bottling Up Rage," *Psychology Today* 7 (July 1973): 24–31.

Butman, R. E. "Anger," in *Baker Encyclopedia of Psychology*, ed. David Benner (Grand Rapids, Mich.: Baker Book House, 1985), 58–60.

Collins, Gary R. *Christian Counseling: A Comprehensive Guide*, rev. (Dallas, Tex.: Word), 1988.

Ellis, Albert. *Anger: How to Live With and Without It.* (Secaucus, N.J.: Citadel Press), 1977.

———. "Techniques of Handling Anger in Marriage," *Journal of Marriage and Family Counseling* 2 (October 1976): 305–315.

Fremont, Suzanne, and Anderson, Wayne. "What Client Behaviors Make Counselors Angry? An Exploratory Study." *Journal of Counseling and Development* 65 (October 1986): 67–70.

Glick, Barry, and Goldstein, Arnold P. "Aggression Replacement Training," *Journal of Counseling and Development* 65 (March 1987): 356–362.

Lerner, Harriet G. *The Dance of Anger.* (New York: Harper and Row), 1985.

# NOTES

1. See the Resources for Christian Counseling series (p. 2 in this volume), edited by Gary R. Collins, Ph.D.
2. Douglas R. Gross and Sharon E. Robinson, "Ethics, Violence, and Counseling: Hear No Evil, See No Evil, Speak No Evil?" *Journal of Counseling and Development* 65 (March 1987): 340–344. Daniel J. Sonkin, "Clairvoyance vs. Common Sense: Therapist's Duty to Warn and Protect," *Violence and Victims* 1 (Spring 1986): 7–22.

## Chapter 1 The Fires Within

1. Suzanne Fremont and Wayne Anderson, "What Client Behaviors Make Counselors Angry? An Exploratory Study," *Journal of Counseling and Development* 65 (October 1986): 67–70.
2. Konrad Lorenz, *On Aggression* (New York: Harcourt, Brace, and World, 1966).
3. *The Dallas Morning News* (Dallas, Tex.) 1 August 1987, H-2.
4. Nan H. Giordana and Jeffrey A. Giordana, "Elder Abuse: A Review of the Literature," *Social Work* (May–June 1984): 232–236. Jane E. Myers and Barbara Shelton, "Abuse and Older Persons: Issues and Implications for Counselors," *Journal of Counseling and Development* 65 (March 1987): 376–380.

5. Keith Farrington, "The Application of Stress Theory to the Study of Family Violence: Principles, Problems, and Prospects," *Journal of Family Violence* 1 (June 1986): 131–147. Grant L. Martin, *Counseling for Family Violence and Abuse* (Waco, Tex.: Word, 1987).

6. Allan Bullock, "The Fuhrer: Portrait of a Dictator," in *Hitler and Nazi Germany,* ed. Robert G. C. Waite (Hinsdale, Ill.: The Dryden Press, 1965), 16.

7. Michael Crichton, *The Terminal Man* (New York: Bantam, 1972).

8. Some sources go further and claim that having enemies is good for people, but the point is debatable. See Bryce L. Boyer, "On Man's Need to Have Enemies: A Psychoanalytic Perspective," *Journal of Psychoanalytic Anthropology* 9 (Spring 1986): 101–120.

9. C. S. Lewis, *A Grief Observed* (New York: Bantam, 1961) and *The Problem of Pain* (New York: Macmillan, 1962).

10. Stanley Schneider and Esti Rimmer, "Adoptive Parents' Hostility Toward Their Adopted Children," *Children and Youth Service Review* 6, no. 4 (1984): 345–352.

11. Sue Stoner and W. Boyd Spencer, "Age and Gender Differences with the Anger Expression Scale," *Educational and Psychological Measurement* 47 (Summer 1987): 487–492.

12. Robert Kellner, Roger J. Wiggins, and Dorothy Pathak, "Distress in Medical and Law Students," *Comprehensive Psychiatry* 27 (May–June 1986): 220–223.

13. Donald Marcus, "The Use and Abuse of Theory in Psychoanalysis," *American Journal of Psychoanalysis* 45 (Spring 1985): 69–75.

14. Douglas H. Ingram, "Madness and the Borderline," *American Journal of Psychoanalysis* 45 (Spring 1985): 69–75.

15. Frederick G. Lopez and Christopher W. Thurman, "A Cognitive-Behavioral Investigation of Anger Among College Students," *Cognitive Therapy and Research* 10 (April 1986): 245–256.

16. S. I. McMillen, *None of These Diseases* (Old Tappan, N.J.: Fleming H. Revell, 1963), 72.

## Chapter 2 Defining Anger and Hostility

1. Jeffrey D. Nason, "The Psychotherapy of Rage: Clinical and Developmental Perspectives," *Contemporary Psychoanalysis* 21 (April 1985): 167–172.

2. The multiple ingredients of the anger response make it a difficult emotion to measure and evaluate, but there are many good tests

available for the measurement of anger. See Richard F. Catlove and Richard E. Braka, "A Test to Measure the Awareness and Expression of Anger," *Psychotherapy and Psychosomatics* 43 (April 1985): 113–119. Jerry L. Deffenbacher, Patricia M. Demm, and Allen D. Brandon, "High General Anger: Correlates and Treatment," *Behavior Research Therapy* 24, no. 4 (1986): 481–489. Robert G. Knight, Ruth A. Ross, Janice I. Collins, and Shana A. Parmenter, "Some Norms, Reliability and Preliminary Validity Data for an S-R Inventory of Anger: the Subjective Anger Scale (SAS)," *Personality and Individual Differences* 6, no. 3 (1985): 331–339. Judith M. Siegel, "The Multidimensional Anger Inventory," *Journal of Personality and Social Psychology* 51 (July 1986): 191–200.

3. S. Crockenberg, "Infant Irritability, Mother Responsiveness, and Social Support Influences on the Security of Infant-Mother Attachment," *Child Development* 52 (1981): 857–865.

4. Allen J. Cahill. "Aggression Revisited: The Value of Anger in Therapy and Other Close Relationships," *Adolescent Psychiatry* 9 (1981): 539–549.

5. Theresa M. Fernandez, "How to Deal With Overt Aggression," *Issues In Mental Health Nursing* 8, no. 1 (1986): 79–83.

6. Ernest H. Johnson and Clifford L. Broman, "The Relationship of Anger Expression to Health Problems Among Black Americans in a National Survey," *Journal of Behavioral Medicine* 10 (April 1987): 103–116. Robert Kellner, Roger J. Wiggins, and Dorothy Pathak, "Distress in Medical and Law Students," *Comprehensive Psychiatry* 27 (May–June 1986): 220–223. Stanley Schneider and Esti Rimmer, "Adoptive Parents' Hostility Toward Their Adopted Children," *Children and Youth Services Review* 6, no. 4 (1984): 345–352.

7. Reuben Fine, "From Hostility to Violence: Some Clinical Observations," *Current Issues in Psychoanalytic Practice* 1 (Summer 1984): 3–17. Jane E. Myers and Barbara Shelton, "Abuse and Older Persons: Issues and Implications for Counselors," *Journal of Counseling and Development* 65 (March 1987): 376–80. Loren H. Roth (Ed.), *Clinical Treatment of the Violent Person* (New York: Guilford, 1987).

8. Albert Ellis, *Anger: How to Live With and Without It* (Secaucus, N.J.: Citadel Press, 1977).

9. Richard P. Walters, *Anger: Yours, Mine and What to Do About It* (Grand Rapids, Mich.: Zondervan, 1981), 13.

10. Ibid., 17.

11. Neil R. Carlson, *Physiology of Behavior, 2nd Ed.* (Boston: Allyn and Bacon, Inc., 1980).

12. See Neil R. Carlson, *Physiology of Behavior, 3rd Ed.* (Boston:

Allyn and Bacon, Inc., 1986), pp. 480–504, for a treatment of the physiology of anger and aggression.

13. V. Ruggieri, N. Sabatini, and G. Muglia, "Relationship Between Emotions and Muscle Tension in Oro-Alimentary Behavior," *Perceptual and Motor Skills* 60 (February 1985): 75–79. H. M. Van der Ploeg, E. T. Van Buuren, and P. Van Brummelen, "The Role of Anger in Hypertension," *Psychotherapy and Psychosomatics* 43 (July 1985): 186–193.

14. Robert W. Frick, "The Prosodic Expression of Anger: Differentiating Threat and Frustration," *Aggressive Behavior* 12, no. 2 (1986): 121–128.

15. Jose Delgado, *Physical Control of the Mind: Toward a Psychocivilized Society* (New York: Harper and Row, 1971), 135.

16. Stephen A. Martin, "Anger as Inner Transformation," *Quadrant* 19 (Spring 1986): 31–45.

17. Michael J. Selby and Robert A. Neimeyer, "Overt and Covert Hostility in Depression," *Psychology: A Quarterly Journal of Human Behavior* 23, no. 1 (1986): 23–25.

18. S. Schacter and J. Singer, "Cognitive, Social and Physiological Determinants of Emotional State," *Psychological Review* 69 (1962): 379–399.

19. Tim LaHaye, *Anger Is a Choice* (Grand Rapids, Mich.: Zondervan, 1982).

20. Cathryn F. Alschuler and Alfred S. Alschuler, "Developing Healthy Responses to Anger: The Counselor's Role," *Journal of Counseling and Development* 63 (September 1984): 26–29.

21. Floyd E. Bloom, Arlyne Lazerson, and Laura Hofstadter, *Brain, Mind, and Behavior* (New York: W. H. Freeman and Co., 1985), 50–51.

22. Zerka T. Moreno, "J. L. Moreno's Concept of Ethical Anger," *Journal of Group Psychotherapy, Psychodrama and Sociometry* 38 (Winter 1986): 145–153.

23. Allen Cahill, "Aggression Revisited."

24. Ibid.

25. Grant L. Martin, *Counseling for Family Violence and Abuse* (Waco, Tex.: Word, 1987).

## Chapter 3 The Causes of Anger

1. Carol Tavris, *Anger: The Misunderstood Emotion* (New York: Simon and Schuster, 1982), 48–52.

2. Konrad Lorenz, *On Aggression* (New York: Harcourt, Brace, and World, 1966).

3. Charles Darwin, *The Expression of the Emotions in Man and Animals* (Chicago: University of Chicago Press, 1965).

4. Andrew Sostek and Richard J. Wyatt, "The Chemistry of Crankiness," *Psychology Today* (October 1981): 120. Henk M. Van der Ploeg, "Emotional States and the Premenstrual Syndrome," *Personality and Individual Differences* 8, no. 1 (1987): 95–100.

5. See Neil R. Carlson, *Physiology of Behavior, 3rd Ed.* (Boston: Allyn and Bacon, Inc., 1986), pp. 480–504 for an in-depth treatment of the physiology of anger and aggression.

6. E. J. Susman, G. Inoff-Germain, E. D. Nottelmann, D. L. Loriaux, G. B. Cutler, Jr., and G. P. Chrousos, "Hormones, Emotional Dispositions, and Aggressive Attributes in Young Adolescents," *Child Development* 58 (1987): 1114–1134.

7. Jeffrey A. Mattes, "Psychopharmacology of Temper Outbursts: A Review," *Journal of Nervous and Mental Disease* 174 (August 1986): 464–470. Adrean Pellegrin, Steven Lippmann, Gary Crump, and Manouchehr Manshadi, "Psychiatric Aspects of Complex Partial Seizures: Case Report," *Journal of Clinical Psychiatry* 45 (June 1984): 269–271.

8. A. Mazur, "Hormones, Aggression, and Dominance in Humans," in *Hormones and Aggressive Behavior*, ed. B. B. Suave (New York: Plenum Press, 1983).

9. Elliot S. Valenstein, *Brain Control* (New York: John Wiley and Sons, 1973), and *The Psychosurgery Debate: Scientific, Legal, and Ethical Perspectives* (San Francisco: W. H. Freeman, 1980).

10. E. M. Cummings, R. J. Iannotti, and C. Zahn-Waxler, "Influence of Conflict Between Adults on the Emotions and Aggression of Young Children," *Developmental Psychology* 21 (1985): 495–507. E. M. Cummings, C. Zahn-Waxler, and M. Radke-Yarrow, "Developmental Changes in Children's Reactions to Anger in the Home," *Journal of Child Psychology and Psychiatry* 25 (1984): 63–74.

11. L. R. Huesmann, L. D. Eron, M. M. Lefkowitz, and L. O. Walder, "Stability of Aggression Over Time and Generations," *Developmental Psychology* 20 (1984): 1120–1134.

12. Some of these different ideas about the Christian life and anger may be responsible for the correlations between certain religious affiliations and hostility. See Charles R. Geist and Cynthia M. Daheim, "Religious Affiliation and Manifest Hostility," *Psychological Reports* 55 (October 1984): 493–494.

13. Eric M. Cottington, Karen A. Matthews, Evelyn Talbott, and Lewis H. Kuller, "Occupational Stress, Surpressed Anger, and Hypertension," *Psychosomatic Medicine* 48 (March–April 1986): 249–260.

14. Doris Hertsgaard and Harriet K. Light, "Anxiety, Depression, and Hostility in Rural Women," *Psychological Reports* 55 (October 1984): 673–674.

15. Harriet K. Light, "Differences in Employed Women's Anxiety, Depression, and Hostility Levels According to Their Career and Family Role Commitment," *Psychological Reports* 55 (August 1984): 290.

16. Michael W. Giles and Arthur Evans, "The Power Approach to Intergroup Hostility," *Journal of Conflict Resolution* 30 (September 1986): 466–486.

17. Keith Farrington, "The Application of Stress Therapy to the Study of Family Violence: Principles, Problems and Prospects," *Journal of Family Violence* 1 (June 1986): 131–147.

18. Michael W. Giles and Arthur Evans, "The Power Approach to Intergroup Hostility," *Journal of Conflict Resolution* 30 (September 1986): 469–486. Robert Kellner, Roger J. Wiggins, and Dorothy Pathak, "Distress in Medical and Law Students," *Comprehensive Psychiatry* 27 (May–June 1986): 220–223.

19. K. E. Moyer, "The Physiology of Violence," *Psychology Today* 7 (July 1973): 35–38.

20. Meira Likierman, "The Function of Anger in Human Conflict," *International Review of Psycho-Analysis* 14, no. 2 (1987): 143–161.

21. Allyson Bond and Malcolm Lader, "A Method to Elicit Aggressive Feelings and Behavior Via Provocation," *Biological Psychology* 22 (February 1986): 69–79.

22. Dolf Zillman and Bryant Jennings, "Effects of Residual Excitation on the Emotional Response to Provocation and Delayed Aggressive Behavior." *Journal of Personality and Social Psychology* 30, no. 6 (1974): 782–791. Dolf Zillman, R. C. Johnson, and K. Day, "Attribution to Apparent Arousal and Proficiency of Recovery From Sympathetic Activation Affecting Excitement Transfer to Aggressive Behavior," *Journal of Experimental Social Psychology* 10 (1974): 503–515.

23. See Carol Tavris, *Anger: The Misunderstood Emotion* (New York: Simon and Schuster, 1982), pp. 169–177 for a discussion of this controversial point.

24. Russell Green, David Stonner, and Gary Shope, "The Facilitation of Aggression by Aggression: Evidence Against the Catharsis

Hypothesis," *Journal of Personality and Social Psychology* 31 (April 1975): 721–726.

25. Yakov M. Epstein, "Crowding, Stress, and Human Behavior," *The Journal of Social Issues* 37 (1981): 126–145.

26. Lawrence K. Wang and Norman C. Pereira, *Air and Noise Pollution Control, vol. 1, Handbook of Environmental Engineering* (Clifton, N.J.: The Humana Press, 1979), 400.

27. Henk M. Van der Ploeg, "Emotional States and the Premenstrual Syndrome."

28. Biovanni A. Fava, "Hostility and Recovery From Melancholia," *Journal of Nervous and Mental Disease,* 174 (July 1986): 414–417.

29. Darwin Dennison, Thomas Preuet, and Michael Affleck, *Alcohol and Behavior* (St. Louis, Mo.: C. V. Mosby, 1980). See also Carol Tavris, *Anger,* pp. 165–169.

30. L. Bryce Boyer, "On Man's Need to Have Enemies: A Psychoanalytic Perspective," *Journal of Psychoanalytic Anthropology* 9 (Spring 1986): 101–120.

31. G. V. Caprara, S. Passerini, C. Pastorelli, and P. Renzi, "Instigating and Measuring Interpersonal Aggression and Hostility: A Methodological Contribution," *Aggressive Behavior* 12, no. 4 (1986): 237–247.

32. Ben Mijuskovic, "Loneliness, Anxiety, Hostility, and Communication," *Child Study Journal* 16, no. 3 (1986): 227–240.

33. Suzanne Retzinger, "The Resentment Process: Videotape Studies," *Psychoanalytic Psychology* 2 (Spring 1985): 129–151.

34. Alan Rossenbaum, "Of Men, Macho, and Marital Violence," *Journal of Family Violence* 1 (June 1986): 121–129.

35. Michael W. Giles and Arthur Evans, "The Power Approach."

36. Norman Rohrer and S. Philip Sutherland, *Facing Anger* (Minneapolis: Augsburg, 1981), 77–90.

37. Yoshiharu Tachibana and Etsushi Hasegawa, "Aggressive Responses of Adolescents to an Hypothetical Frustrative Situation," *Psychological Reports* 58 (February 1986): 111–118.

38. Reuben Fine, "From Hostility to Violence: Some Clinical Observations," *Current Issues in Psychoanalytic Practice* 1 (Summer 1984): 3–17.

39. Mary L. Biaggio, "Anger Arousal and Personality Characteristics," *Journal of Personality and Social Psychology* 39, no. 2 (1980): 352–356.

40. Y. Tachibana and E. Hasegawa, "Aggressive Responses of Adolescents."

41. Bernard Weiner, James Amirkhan, Valerie Folkes, and Julie Verette, "An Attributional Analysis of Excuse Giving: Studies of a Naive Theory of Emotion," *Journal of Personality and Social Psychology* 52 (February 1987): 316–324.

42. Michael S. Steinberg and Kenneth A. Dodge, "Attributional Bias in Aggressive Adolescent Boys and Girls," *Journal of Social and Clinical Psychology* 4, no. 1 (1983): 312–321.

43. Sara B. Moss and Jerry L. Whiteman, "An Analysis of Alcoholics' Perception of Hostility Before and After Treatment," *Journal of Substance Abuse Treatment,* 2, no. 2 (1985): 107–111.

44. Bert Ghezzi, *The Angry Christian* (Ann Arbor, Mich.: Servant Books, 1980).

45. C. S. Lewis, *The Great Divorce* (New York: Macmillan, 1946), 92–93.

## Chapter 4 How Not to Deal with Anger

1. David W. Augsburger, *Anger and Assertiveness in Pastoral Care* (Philadelphia: Fortress Press, 1979).

2. Neil C. Warren, *Make Anger Your Ally* (Garden City, New York: Doubleday, 1985).

3. Harriet G. Lerner, *The Dance of Anger* (New York: Harper and Row, 1985).

4. Leonard Berkowitz, "The Case for Bottling Up Rage," *Psychology Today* 7 (July 1973): 24–31.

5. See Carol Tavris, *Anger: The Misunderstood Emotion* (New York: Simon and Schuster, 1982), pp. 169–177 for a discussion of this.

6. Eric M. Cottington, Karen A. Matthews, Evelyn Talbott, and Lewis H. Kuller, "Occupational Stress, Suppressed Anger, and Hypertension," *Psychosomatic Medicine* (March–April 1986): 249–260. H. M. Van der Ploeg, E. T. Van Buuren, and P. Van Brummelen, "The Role of Anger in Hypertension," *Psychotherapy and Psychosomatics* 43 (July 1985): 186–193.

7. V. Ruggieri, N. Sabatini, and G. Muglia, "Relationship Between Emotions and Muscle Tension in Oro-Alimentary Behavior," *Perceptual and Motor Skills* 60 (February 1985): 75–79.

8. J. M. MacDougall, T. M. Dembroski, J. E. Dimsdale, and T. P. Hackett, "Components of Type A, Hostility, and Anger-in: Further Relationships to Angiographic Findings," *Health Psychology* 4, no. 2 (1985): 137–152.

9. Logan Wright, "Type A Behavior Pattern and Coronary Artery Disease: Quest for the Active Ingredients and the Elusive Mechanism," *American Psychologist* 43 (January 1988): 2–14.

10. William Blake, "The Poison Tree," in *The Literature of England, vol. 2, 5th Ed.* ed. George K. Anderson and William E. Buckler (Glenview, Ill.: Scott Foresman and Co., 1966), 147.

11. Charles Darwin, *The Expression of Emotions in Man and Animals* (Chicago: University of Chicago Press, 1965). Sigmund Freud, *A General Introduction to Psychoanalysis* (New York: Washington Square Press, 1961). Konrad Lorenz, *On Aggression* (New York: Harcourt, Brace, and World, 1966). Desmond Morris, *The Naked Ape* (New York: Dell, 1969). E. O. Wilson, *Sociobiology, The New Synthesis* (Cambridge: Harvard University Press, 1975).

12. Carol Tavris, "On the Wisdom of Counting to Ten: Personal and Social Dangers of Anger Expression," *Review of Personality and Social Psychology* 5 (1984): 170–191.

13. Seymour Feshback, "Reconceptualizations of Anger: Some Research Perspectives," *Journal of Social and Clinical Psychology* 4, no. 2 (1986): 123–132.

14. Harriet Lerner, *The Dance of Anger.*

15. Carol Tavris, "On the Wisdom of Counting to Ten."

16. Ibid., *Anger,* 123–131.

17. Ibid., 133–135.

## Chapter 5  Slow to Anger: Holding Anger Back

1. Cathryn F. Alschuler and Alfred S. Alschuler, "Developing Healthy Responses to Anger: The Counselor's Role," *Journal of Counseling and Development* 63 (September 1984): 26–29.

2. Two writers who argue against turning the other cheek are Albert Ellis, *Anger: How to Live With and Without It* (Secaucus, N.J.: Citadel Press, 1977) and Harriet Lerner, *The Dance of Anger* (New York: Harper and Row, 1985).

3. Barry Glick and Arnold P. Goldstein, "Aggression Replacement Training," *Journal of Counseling and Development* 65 (March 1987): 356–362.

4. Betsey Bensen, "Anger Management Training," *Psychiatric Aspects of Mental Retardation Reviews* 5 (October 1986): 51–55. Betsey Benson, Christine Rice, and S. Vincent Miranti, "Effects of Anger Management Training with Mentally Retarded Adults in Group Treatment," *Journal of Consulting and Clinical Psychology*

54 (October 1986): 728–729. R. E. Emery, "Interparent Conflict and the Children of Discord and Divorce," *Psychological Bulletin* 92 (1982): 310–330. Charles T. Ruby, "Defusing the Hostile Ex-Offender: Rational Behavior Training," *Emotional First Aid: A Journal of Crisis Intervention* 1 (Spring 1984): 17–22. Murray Scher and Mark Stevens, "Men and Violence," *Journal of Counseling and Development* 65 (March 1987): 351–355.

    5. Alexandra G. Kaplan, "Women and Anger in Psychotherapy," *Women and Therapy* 2 (Summer–Fall 1983): 29–40.

    6. Murray Scher and Mark Stevens, "Men and Violence."

    7. Eva L. Feindler, Randolph B. Ecton, Deborah Kingsley, and Dennis R. Dubey, "Group Anger-Control Training for Institutionalized Psychiatric Male Adolescents," *Behavior Therapy* 17 (March 1986): 109–123. Denise E. Wilfley, Carole J. Rodon, and Wayne P. Anderson, "Angry Women Offenders: Case Study of a Group," *International Journal of Offender Therapy and Comparative Criminology* 30, no. 1 (1986): 41–51.

    8. Jerry L. Deffenbacher, Patricia M. Dennison, and Allen D. Brandon, "High General Anger: Correlates and Treatment," *Behavior Research Therapy* 24, no. 4 (1986): 480–489. Kenneth Hart, Anxiety Management Training and Anger Control for Type A Individuals," *Journal of Behavior Therapy and Experimental Psychiatry* 15 (June 1984): 133–139. Susan Hazaleus and Jerry Deffenbacher, "Relaxation and Cognitive Treatments of Anger," *Journal of Counseling and Clinical Psychology* 54 (April 1986): 222–226. H. M. Van der Ploeg, E. T. Van Buuren, and P. Van Brummelen, "The Role of Anger in Hypertension," *Psychotherapy and Psychosomatics* 43 (July 1985): 186–193.

    9. Two good sources are Albert Ellis, *Anger: How to Live With and Without It* (Secaucus, N.J.: Citadel Press, 1977), and Albert Bandura, "Learning and Behavioral Theories of Aggression," in *Violence,* ed. Kutash, *et al.* (San Francisco: Jossey Bass, 1978).

    10. Jane Myers and Barbara Shelton, "Abuse and Older Persons: Issues and Implications for Counselors," *Journal of Counseling and Development* 65 (March 1987): 376–380.

    11. Jerry Deffenbacher, A. Deborah, Robert Stark, and James Hogg, "Cognitive Relaxation and Social Skills Interventions in the Treatment of General Anger," *Journal of Counseling Psychology* 34 (April 1987): 171–176.

    12. Arlo Compaan, "Anger, Denial, and the Healing of Memories," *Journal of Psychology and Christianity* 4 (Summer 1985): 83–85.

13. Richard P. Walters, *Anger: Yours, Mine and What to Do About It* (Grand Rapids, Mich.: Zondervan, 1981), 69.

14. Seymour Feshback, "Reconceptualizations of Anger: Some Research Perspectives," *Journal of Social and Clinical Psychology* 4, no. 2 (1986): 123–132.

15. Charles T. Ruby, "Defusing the Hostile Ex-Offender."

16. Albert Ellis, *Anger.*

17. Ibid.

18. Suzanne Retzinger, "The Resentment Process: Videotape Studies," *Psychoanalytic Psychology* 2 (Spring 1985): 129–151.

19. Richard P. Fitzgibbons, "The Cognitive and Emotive Uses of Forgiveness in the Treatment of Anger," *Psychotherapy* 23 (Winter 1986): 629–633.


## Chapter 6 Expressing Anger Properly

1. Eric M. Cottington, Karen A. Matthews, Evelyn Talbott, and Lewis H. Kuller, "Occupational Stress, Suppressed Anger, and Hypertension," *Psychosomatic Medicine* 48 (March–April 1986): 249–260. Kenneth E. Hart, "Anxiety Management Training and Anger Control for Type A Individuals," *Journal of Behavior Therapy and Experimental Psychiatry* 15 (June 1984): 133–139. James M. MacDougall, Theodore M. Dembroski, Joel E. Dinsdale, and Thomas P. Hackett, "Components of Type A Hostility and Anger-in: Further Relationships to Angiographic Findings," *Health Psychology* 4, no. 2 (1985): 137–152. Logan Wright, "Type A Behavior Pattern and Coronary Artery Disease: Quest for the Active Ingredients and the Elusive Mechanism," *American Psychologist* 43 (January 1988): 2–14.

2. Betsey A. Benson, "Anger Management Training," *Psychiatric Aspects of Mental Retardation Reviews* 5 (October 1986): 51–55. John E. Lochman and John F. Curry, "Effects of Social Problem-Solving Training and Self-Instruction with Aggressive Boys," *Journal of Clinical Child Psychology* 15 (Summer 1986): 159–164.

3. Allen J. Cahill, "Aggression Revisited: The Value of Anger in Therapy and Other Close Relationships," *Adolescent Psychiatry* 9 (1981): 539–549.

4. Paul E. Baer, "Conflict Management in the Family: The Impact of Paternal Hypertension," *Advances in Family Intervention, Assessment and Theory* 3 (1983): 161–184. Betsey A. Benson, Christine

Johnson Rice, and S. Vincent Miranti, "Effects of Anger Management Training with Mentally Retarded Adults in Group Treatment," *Journal of Consulting and Clinical Psychology* 54 (1986): 728–729. R. E. Emery, "Interparent Conflict and the Children of Discord and Divorce," *Psychological Bulletin* 92 (1982): 310–330. Barry Glick and Arnold P. Goldstein, "Aggression Replacement Training," *Journal of Counseling and Development* 65 (March 1987): 356–362.

5. Richard P. Walters, *Anger: Yours and Mine and What to Do About It* (Grand Rapids, Mich.: Zondervan, 1981), 46–47.

6. Cathryn F. Alschuler and Alfred S. Alschuler, "Developing Healthy Responses to Anger: The Counselor's Role," *Journal of Counseling and Development* 63 (September 1984): 26–29.

7. O. H. Bower, "Mood and Memory," *American Psychologist* 36 (1981): 129–148.

8. Alschuler and Alschuler, "Developing Healthy Responses to Anger."

9. Dennis C. Breidenbach, "Behavioral Skills Training for Students: A Preventive Program," *Social Work in Education* 6 (Summer 1984): 231–240. Barry Glick and Arnold P. Goldstein, "Aggression Replacement Training."

10. Kathleen L. Davis, "Teaching Counselor Trainees to Respond Consistently to Different Aspects of Anger," *Journal of Counseling Psychology* 32 (October 1985): 580–588. Conway F. Saylor, Betsey Benson, and Lynne Einhaus, "Evaluation of Anger Management Program for Aggressive Boys in Inpatient Treatment," *Journal of Child and Adolescent Psychotherapy* 2, no. 1 (1985): 5–15.

11. David W. Augsburger, *Anger and Assertiveness in Pastoral Care* (Philadelphia: Fortress Press, 1979).

12. Lewis B. Smedes, *Forgive and Forget: Healing the Hurts We Don't Deserve* (New York: Harper and Row, 1984).

13. Richard P. Fitzgibbons, "The Cognitive and Emotive Uses of Forgiveness in the Treatment of Anger," *Psychotherapy* 23 (Winter 1986): 629–633.

14. Ray Burwick, *Anger: Defusing the Bomb* (Wheaton, Ill.: Tyndale House, 1981), 85–86.

## Chapter 7 Counseling Anger in Marriage

1. "Surgeon General's Workshop on Violence: Recommendations on Spouse Abuse," *Response to the Victimization of Women and Children* 9, no. 1 (1986), 19–21. Murray Straus, Richard Gelles, and

Suzanne Steinmetz, *Behind Closed Doors: Violence in the American Family* (Garden City, New York: Doubleday, Anchor, 1980). Lenore Walker, *The Battered Woman Syndrome* (New York: Springer, 1984). The reader will find the following helpful in counseling the anger in spouse-abuse cases. Jeanne P. Deschner and John S. McNeil, "Results of Anger-Control Training for Battering Couples," *Journal of Family Violence* 1 (June 1986): 121–129. Murray Scher and Mark Stevens, "Men and Violence," *Journal of Counseling and Development* 65 (March 1987): 351–355. Michael Waldo, "Also Victims: Understanding and Treating Men Arrested for Spouse Abuse," *Journal of Counseling and Development* 65 (March 1987): 385–388.

2. Doris Hertsgaard and Harriet K. Light, "Anxiety, Depression, and Hostility in Rural Women," *Psychological Reports* 55 (October 1984): 673–674.

3. Claudeen Cline-Naffziger, "Women's Lives and Frustration, Oppression, and Anger." Alexandra G. Kaplan, "Women and Anger in Psychotherapy," *Women and Therapy* 2 (Summer–Fall 1983): 29–40.

4. Harriet K. Light, "Differences in Employed Women's Anxiety, Depression, and Hostility Levels According to Their Career and Family Role Commitment," *Psychological Reports* 55 (August 1984): 290.

5. Patricia Noller, "Misunderstandings in Marital Communication: A Study of Couples' Nonverbal Communication," *Journal of Personality and Social Psychology* 39, no. 6 (1980): 1135–1148.

6. Albert Ellis, "Techniques of Handling Anger in Marriage," *Journal of Marriage and Family Counseling* 2 (October 1976): 305–515.

7. George J. Steinfeld, "Spouse Abuse: Clinical Implications of Research on the Control of Aggression," *Journal of Family Violence* 1 (June 1986): 197–208.

8. Lawrence J. Crabb, *The Marriage Builder* (Grand Rapids, Mich.: Zondervan, 1982).

9. Carol Tavris, *Anger: The Misunderstood Emotion* (New York: Simon and Schuster, 1982), 226.

10. Lawrence Crabb, *The Marriage Builder*.

11. Ibid.

## Chapter 8 Counseling Anger in Children

1. Paul Welter, "Children as Teachers of Forgiveness," in *Parents and Children*, ed. Jay Kesler, Ron Beers, and LaVonne Neff (Wheaton, Ill.: Victor Books, 1986), 627–628.

2. Carolyn Uhlinger, "Conflicts Between Children," *Child Development* 58 (1987): 283–305.

3. Paul Welter, "Children as Teachers of Forgiveness," 628.

4. Susan Crockenberg, "Predictors and Correlates of Anger Toward and Primitive Control of Toddlers by Adolescent Mothers," *Child Development* 58 (August–December 1987): 964–975.

5. Ken Rotenberg, "Causes, Intensity, Motives, and Consequences of Children's Anger from Self Reports," *Journal of Genetic Psychology* 146 (March 1985): 101–106.

6. Peggy Miller and Linda L. Sperry, "The Socialization of Anger and Aggression," *Merrill-Palmer Quarterly* 32 (January 1987): 1–31.

7. E. M. Cummings, R. J. Iannotti, and C. Zahn-Waxler, "Influence of Conflict Between Adults on the Emotions and Aggression of Young Children," *Developmental Psychology* 21 (1985): 495–507. E. M. Cummings, C. Zahn-Waxler, and M. Radke-Yarrow, "Developmental Changes in Children's Reactions to Anger in the Home," *Journal of Child Psychology and Psychiatry* 25 (1984): 63–74.

8. Mark E. Cummings, "Background Anger in Early Childhood," *Child Development* 58 (August 1987): 976–984.

9. Katherine Covell and Rona Abramovitch, "Understanding Emotion in the Family: Children's and Parents' Attributions of Happiness, Sadness, and Anger," *Child Development* 58 (August 1987): 985–991.

10. Susan Crockenberg, "Predictors and Correlates of Anger."

11. Susan Crockenberg, "Toddlers' Reactions to Maternal Anger," *Merrill-Palmer Quarterly* 31 (October 1985): 361–373.

12. David W. Shantz, "Conflict, Aggression, and Peer Status: An Observational Study," *Child Development* 57 (1986): 1322–1332.

13. Elizabeth J. Susman, Gail Inoff-Germain, Editha D. Nottelmann, D. Lynn Loriaux, Gordon B. Cutler, and Gerze P. Chrousos, "Hormones, Emotional Dispositions, and Aggressive Attrributes in Young Adolescents," *Child Development* 58 (1987): 1114–1134.

14. Michael S. Steinberg and Kenneth A. Dodge, "Attributional Bias in Aggressive Adolescent Boys and Girls," *Journal of Social and Clinical Psychology* 4, no. 1 (1983): 312–321.

15. Samuel Vuchiwich, "Starting and Stopping Spontaneous Family Conflicts," *Journal of Marriage and the Family* 49 (August 1987): 591–601.

16. Gail M. Price, "Fathers Provoke Not Your Children: A Study of Rage in a Sexually Abused Girl," *Journal of Psychology and Christianity* 4 (Summer 1985): 71–75.

17. Sharlene A. Wolchik, Sanford L. Buauer, and Irwin N. Sandler, "Maternal vs. Joint Custody: Children's Postseparation Experiences and Adjustment," *Journal of Clinical Child Psychology* 14 (Spring 1985): 5–10.

18. Susan Crockenberg, "Predictors and Correlates of Anger."

19. Ernest N. Jouriles, Juliana Barling, and Daniel K. O'Learly, "Predicting Child Behavior Problems in Maritally Violent Families," *Journal of Abnormal Child Psychology* 15 (June 1987): 165–173.

20. Justin D. Call, "Child Abuse and Neglect in Infancy: Sources of Hostility Within the Parent-Infant Dyad and Disorders of Attachment in Infancy," *Child Abuse and Neglect* 8, no. 2 (1984): 185–202.

21. Carol Tavris, *Anger: The Misunderstood Emotion* (New York: Simon and Schuster, 1982), 136.

22. For further reading on anger-management training programs for children see Dennis C. Breidenbach, "Behavioral Skills Training for Students: A Preventive Program," *Social Work in Education* 6 (Summer 1984): 231–240, and Barry Glick and Arnold P. Goldstein, "Aggression Replacement Training," *Journal of Counseling and Development* 65 (March 1987): 356–362.

23. Ross Campbell, *How to Really Know Your Child* (Wheaton, Ill.: Victor Books, 1987). *How to Really Love Your Teenager* (Wheaton, Ill.: Victor Books, 1981).

## Chapter 9 Counseling and Anger at Self

1. Dona M. Kagan and Rose L. Squires, "Compulsive Eating, Dieting, Stress, and Hostility Among College Students," *Journal of College Student Personnel* 25 (May 1984): 213–220.

2. Roger Farmer, "Hostility and Deliberate Self-Poisoning: The Role of Depression," *British Journal of Psychiatry* 150 (May 1987): 607–614. Ben Mijuskovic, "Loneliness, Anxiety, Hostility, and Communication," *Child Study Journal* 16, no. 3 (1986): 227–240.

3. Justin D. Call, "Child Abuse and Neglect in Infancy: Sources of Anxiety Within the Parent-Infant Dyad and Disorders of Attachment in Infancy," *Child Abuse and Neglect* 8, no. 2 (1984): 185–202. Peter H. Neidig, Dale H. Friedman, and Barbara S. Collins, "Attitudinal Characteristics of Males Who Have Engaged in Spouse Abuse," *Journal of Family Violence* 1 (September 1986): 223–233. Michael Waldo, "Also Victims: Understanding and Treating Men Arrested for Spouse Abuse," *Journal of Counseling and Development* 65 (March 1987): 385–388.

4. Murray Scher and Mark Stevens, "Men and Violence," *Journal of Counseling and Development* 65 (March 1987): 351–355.

5. Susan Crockenberg, "Predictors and Correlates of Anger Toward and Punitive Control of Toddlers by Adolescent Mothers," *Child Development* 58 (August 1987): 964–965.

6. David Carlson, *Counseling and Self-Esteem*, vol. 13, *Resources for Christian Counseling* (Waco, Tex.: Word, 1988).

7. G. V. Caprara, S. Passerini, C. Pastorelli, and P. Renzi, "Instigating and Measuring Interpersonal Aggression and Hostility: A Methodological Contribution," *Aggressive Behavior* 12, no. 4 (1986): 237–247.

8. Ibid.

9. Kenneth A. Dodge and Daniel R. Somberg, "Hostile Attributional Biases Among Aggressive Boys Are Exacerbated Under Conditions of Threat to Self," *Child Development* 58 (February 1987): 213–224.

10. S. Bruce Narramore, *No Condemnation* (Grand Rapids, Mich.: Zondervan, 1984).

11. Alexandra G. Kaplan, "Women and Anger in Psychotherapy," *Women and Therapy* 2 (Summer–Fall 1983): 29–40.

**Chapter 10 Counseling and Anger at God**

1. Sidney Zisook and Stephen R. Shuchter, "The First Four Years of Widowhood," *Psychiatric Annals* 16 (May 1986): 288–294.

2. A good source for counseling bereaved individuals including their anger is Sherry E. Johnson, *After a Child Dies: Counseling Bereaved Families* (New York: Springer, 1987).

3. George H. Pollock, "Childhood Sibling Loss: A Family Tragedy," *Psychiatric Annals* 16 (May 1986): 309–314.

4. Mary K. O'Neil, William J. Lance, and Stanley J. Freeman, "Loss and Depression: A Controversial Look," *Journal of Nervous and Mental Disease* (June 1987): 354–359.

5. For some helpful suggestions, see Stephen R. Shuchter and Sidney Zisook, "Treatment of Spousal Bereavement: A Multidimensional Approach," *Psychiatric Annals* 16 (May 1986): 295–305.

6. C. S. Lewis, *The Problem of Pain* (New York: Macmillan, 1962).

7. Ibid., *A Grief Observed* (New York: Bantam, 1961).

8. Harold S. Kushner, *When Bad Things Happen to Good People* (New York: Schocken Books, 1981).

9. Philip Yancey, *Where Is God When It Hurts?* (Grand Rapids, Mich.: Zondervan, 1977).

## Chapter 11 Preventing Anger

1. Dennis C. Breidenbach, "Behavioral Skills Training for Students: A Preventive Program," *Social Work in Education* 6 (Summer 1984): 231–240. Barry Glick and Arnold P. Goldstein, "Aggression Replacement Training," *Journal of Counseling and Development* 65 (March 1987): 356–362.

2. Dennis C. Breidenbach, "Behavioral Skills Training for Students."

3. Cathryn F. Alschuler and Alfred S. Alschuler, "Developing Healthy Responses to Anger: The Counselor's Role," *Journal of Counseling and Development* 63 (September 1984): 26–29.

4. Toby Katz, "Hostile Audience: Proceed With Caution!" *Training and Development Journal* 38 (February 1984): 78–83.

5. How counselors deal with their own angers toward their clients can be a model for their counselees. See Suzanne Fremont and Wayne Anderson, "What Client Behaviors Make Counselors Angry? An Exploratory Study," *Journal of Counseling and Development* 65 (October 1986): 67–70.

6. John M. McDonagh, "Working Through Resistance by Prayer and the Gift of Knowledge: A Case Study of Anger," *Journal of Psychology and Christianity* 4 (Summer 1985): 26–28.

# INDEX

Adolescents, anger in, 131
Adrenaline, 30, 31
Alcohol, 53–54
Anger: biblical words for,
    29–30; components of, 27,
    28–29, 31–33; definition of,
    26–27; negative results of,
    21–22, 37–38; theories of,
    46–49, types of, 18–19, 21
Anger as resolution, 90–91
Anger as sin, 29, 40–41
Anger at God, 20–21
Anger at self, 20–21, 135–36,
    144
Anger cliches, 17, 34
Anger energy, 34–35
Anger expression, 93
Anger of God, 41, 148–50;
    biblical examples of, 152;
    expression of, 153;
    limitations of, 155
Augsburger, David, 97

Biology of anger, 28, 30–31,
    47
Bitterness, 38–40
Blake, William (poet),
    68–69

Catharsis, 48
Child abuse, 15
Children's anger, 50–51,
    119–20, 128–29; causes of,
    123; as communication,
    125; at parents, 126
Cognitive theory, 48–49
Communication, 109, 171
Competition, 52, 172
Confession, 98
Confrontation, 96–97
Crabb, Larry, 112, 115–16
Crowds, 53

Darwin, Charles, 46
David, 35, 36

Depression, 136
Divorce, 126

Elderly abuse, 15
Emotional stress, 170
Ethical anger, 35
Ethological theory, 46–47

Forgiveness, 99, 102; steps of, 100–01; results of, 103–04; of self, 146–47
Freudian theory, 48
Frustration, 57

Guilt feelings, 32, 57

Humility, 99, 139–40, 144
Hypertension, 68

Irrational beliefs, 82–83
Irritations, 84–85

Jesus: anger of, 41; teachings on anger, 75–77, 94
Job stress, 51

!Kung people, 46
Kushner, Rabbi Harold, 159

Laughter, 55
Lerner, Harriet, 71
Lewis, C. S., 18, 151
Lorenz, Konrad, 46

Marital anger, 106–07, 117–18; causes of, 108–10
Meir, Golda, 95
Mind-set, 68–69, 113, 167
Moreno, J. L., 35
Moses, 35

Noise, 53

Parents, 122
Passive-aggression, 51, 65–66

Pastor's anger, 20
Peace of mind, 87, 166
Perfectionism, 55–56
Physical health, 53
Power struggle, 52, 55
Prayer, 118, 154
Prayer partner, 174
Predispositions to anger, 44–45
Prevention of anger, 164–67, 173
Premenstrual syndrome, 53

Racial hostilities, 55
Rage, 63, 69–71
Rejection, 58
Relationships, 86, 172
Resentment, 63–64, 68–69
Righteous anger, 91, 174–75

Self-centeredness, 60
Self-confrontation, 145
Self-esteem, 52, 54–55, 137–38, 141, 170; biblical teaching on, 139
Self-sufficiency, 54
Sermon on the Mount, 75–76
Sexual abuse, 103
Sibling rivalry, 124
Sin nature, 59–60
Sports, 52
Spouse abuse, 15
Suffering, 156–58
Suppression of anger, 66–68

Tavris, Carol, 113
Temper tantrum: in children, 130; in adults, 132
Thought control, 79–80
Tongue, 171

Wife batterers, 55

## Mark P. Cosgrove, Ph.D.

Mark P. Cosgrove is professor of psychology and chairman of the psychology department of Taylor University, Upland, Indiana, where he has served on the faculty since 1976. A graduate of Creighton University, he earned the M.S. and Ph.D. degrees in psychology from Purdue University. Dr. Cosgrove has published a number of articles and is the author or co-author of four books on the integration of psychology and Christianity, including *The Essence of Human Nature* and *B. F. Skinner's Behaviorism: An Analysis.* He and his wife Jo Ann have three sons—Walker, Robert and Preston—and reside in Upland, Indiana.